Jonathan Hassell
Learning PowerShell

W0016815

Jonathan Hassell

Learning PowerShell

First Edition

ISBN 978-1-5015-1532-3
e-ISBN (PDF) 978-1-5015-0667-3
e-ISBN (EPUB) 978-1-5015-0661-1

Library of Congress Cataloging-in-Publication Data
A CIP catalog record for this book has been applied for at the Library of Congress.

Bibliographic information published by the Deutsche Nationalbibliothek
The Deutsche Nationalbibliothek lists this publication in the Deutsche Nationalbibliografie;
detailed bibliographic data are available on the Internet at http://dnb.dnb.de.

© 2017 Walter de Gruyter Inc., Boston/Berlin
Printing and binding: CPI book GmbH, Leck
♾ Printed on acid-free paper
Printed in Germany

www.degruyter.com

To Sara, Jacob, and Mason, for you all are the reason I do everything.

Acknowledgements

Writing a book is not exactly something you do overnight or even alone. This will mark my eighth trip down the authoring road, so I know well the team effort it takes to get from a blank page to a polished, published work. Even through I released the first version of this book through my own company, many folks helped to shape that manuscript into the text you're reading today. Thanks to Jeff Pepper and Megan Lester at De Gruyter for showing an interest in this work and all of the production staff for shepherding this project through the process. (Any errors that remain in the book are mine and mine alone.) Thanks to Jason Gilmore for doing a sanity check review on the original manuscript, and thanks to Len Epp and the Leanpub team for their contributions and support. And last but not least, a special thanks to my family. I hope I've done you proud.

Contents

Chapter 1
Getting Started and Setting Up

Welcome to *Learning PowerShell*! In this chapter, my main goal is to get you set up and ready to start working. To do so, there are a couple of applications you need to learn about and just a couple of notes I'd like to clear up so that you aren't super confused as you start your march to PowerShell mastery.

Valid Platforms and Versions

PowerShell is designed, of course, to be run on all kinds of machines. In fact, the broader support that PowerShell has, the more likely more developers and hardware makers will adopt the language and incorporate it into their own offerings. It is sort of like a self-fulfilling prophecy, in that the more systems that support PowerShell, the more people and systems will want to use PowerShell, which will make even more systems use PowerShell, and so on.

The two most important things to note about the systems you will use to learn PowerShell is which version of PowerShell you will be using, and what platform your computer (or computers as we get more advanced, since we will be trying to script actions and fire commands across large swaths of machines simultaneously) is.

To determine what version of PowerShell you have, all you need to do is open PowerShell and type a single command. Click the Start menu and start typing "powershell" and you should come across "Windows PowerShell." Click that to open it up and you should see what looks like a text-based prompt. Type the following at that prompt:

```
$PSVersionTable.PSVersion
```

It should spit out a little table with four columns: Major, Minor, Build, and Revision. All you care about is the number in the Major column. That is the column that tells you what version you have. You need to have version 3 or higher to get the most from this book. PowerShell updates are free to download, so if you find you are using a version earlier than version 3, go to Microsoft.com and search for PowerShell, and you'll find some pages that will help you download the new version and get it installed on your system. It just so happens that PowerShell 3 was a pretty big release, and a lot of new features were added to make life easier in a

DOI 10.1515/9781501506673-001

lot of ways, so it is a good baseline we can use for teaching. As I write this, Windows 10 ships with PowerShell version 5, so there have definitely been later revisions of the language, but they have mostly added more advanced features and scripting support and almost nothing has changed for the total beginner. So get to version 3 and then you are set on this point.

As far as your system's platform goes, this is only a little bit trickier to figure out. Computing as we know it today is divided into a couple of camps:

- **x64**: 64-bit computing is pretty much the cutting edge of what you can buy today and really enables you to have gobs of RAM. PowerShell generally assumes you are running 64-bit, and pretty much everything you come across in this course or even on the Internet as you start searching for command and scripting ideas and then borrowing them (ahem) for personal use will work. If you have bought a machine within the past five years, then you have a 64-bit machine, and correspondingly you have nothing to worry about.

- **x86**: this is the platform of yesteryear. If you are running on machines purchased before 2007, then you probably are still 32-bit. If you have less than 4 GB of RAM, there is a chance that you are running a 32-bit operating system. PowerShell still works on this platform, but some more advanced stuff may run differently and some commands actually may not work at all. It is still plenty good enough to learn PowerShell with, so do not think in order to go any further you have to buy a whole new PC! Yours will work fine. All you need to do is use the x86 version of the Windows PowerShell console or the Windows PowerShell Integrated Scripting Environment. You will know which one because it specifically has "(x86)" in the title. But do not use this version unless you must.

Again, to keep it simple, use the 64-bit version of PowerShell (the one that does NOT have the (x86) designator in the title) unless you have a really specific reason why you need to use the 32-bit version.

Are you on version 3 and you know which platform version of PowerShell to use? Fantastic! Let's move on.

Two Important PowerShell Tools

To use PowerShell, there are basically two avenues you can take: you can use a console window, which is just a place to type in commands and read the responses the system sends back to you, or you can use a graphical tool that lets you type in the same commands but also has a few more features to make it a little easier to explore PowerShell. The two are not mutually exclusive; you can use either or both depending on the task. Let me show you each of them, and while I am taking you through each of the utilities I will mention some sample situations in which each of them would be useful and when to think about using the other one.

The PowerShell Integrated Scripting Environment (ISE)

I think the easiest way to get started with PowerShell is to have a little bit of hand holding, and the Windows PowerShell Integrated Scripting Environment, which you will sometimes see labeled as the Windows PowerShell ISE, is the best way without spending any money. Figure 1.1 shows the way the Windows PowerShell ISE looks out of the box.

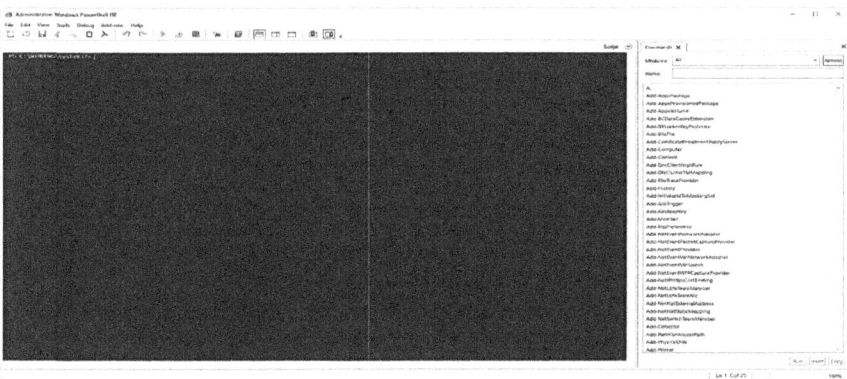

Figure 1.1: The default look of the Windows PowerShell ISE.

The main idea behind the ISE is to help you build scripts. You can do it in a friendlier, more aesthetically pleasing environment with a lot of help both in your face and behind the scenes, too. It gives you the console window, which is the big blue area that looks like a DOS prompt and kind of has the same look as the window you opened earlier in this chapter to check the version of PowerShell you are running. On the right, it gives you some graphical help in finding and selecting the best commands to use for any job. However, there is also the scripting pane, which you can turn on by going to the View menu and selecting Scripting Pane. Here, in Figure 1.2, is what that adds to the equation.

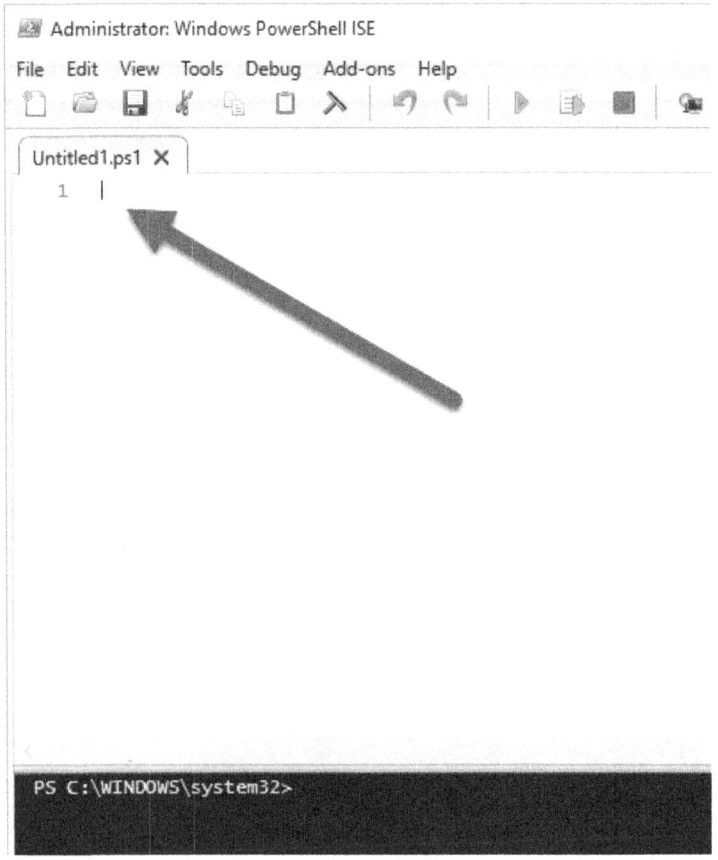

Figure 1.2: Adding the scripting pane to the Windows PowerShell ISE.

IntelliSense

It is easy to get started with PowerShell using the ISE because it includes some cool features. The best one for beginners is called IntelliSense, and it is like a PowerShell expert standing behind you, looking over your shoulder and helping you pick the right commands for the job. You can try it easily. Just type in

```
Get-Process
```

...into the scripting pane. You will see that as you start typing, the ISE will help-fully pop up a menu of choices that you can use. I have put an example of this in Figure 1.3. If you see one you like, you can simply hit the Tab key, and the ISE will automatically type in the rest of the command for you. To scroll up and down in the list, you can use the arrow keys if you do not want your fingers leaving the keyboard, or you can use the mouse to scroll up and down via the mouse's center wheel or via the up and down buttons.

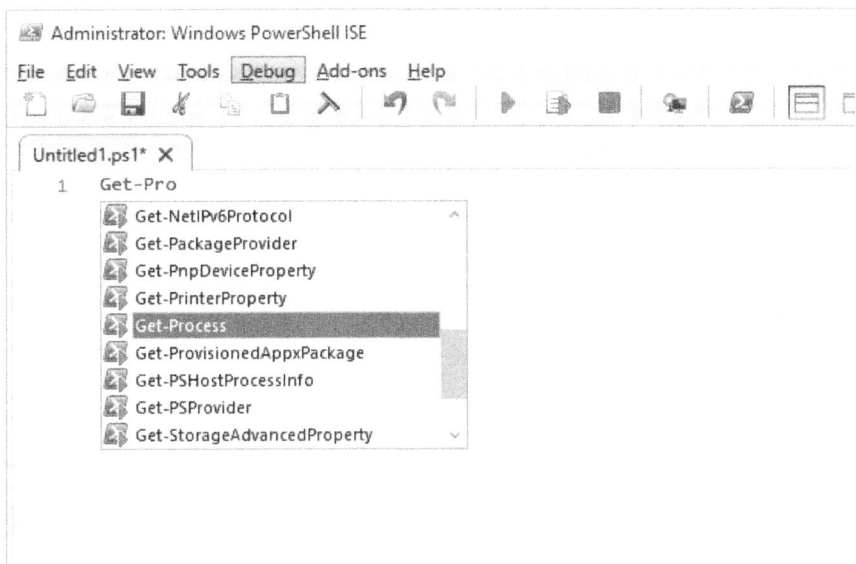

Figure 1.3: IntelliSense in the Windows PowerShell ISE will help you narrow the universe of commands from which you can choose.

Once you have finished the command you want to run, either hit the F5 key on your keyboard or click the green right arrow up in the toolbar that is a little to the right of the Help menu. What you have written will run in the console window, and you will see the results there, too.

The IntelliSense feature also works for the potatoes part of the command, too (the command itself is the meat, but the potatoes are all the stuff that follows the command; you'll learn about these in the next chapter). For instance, and just take my word for this now, there is a command called Get-EventLog that will look inside the event logs that Windows keeps to track what happens on your system. Part of that command is specifying which event log you want to look at, and since Windows can generate and log a lot of events, you probably are ever interested only in a pretty small subset of all the events available in any one event log. So again, just taking my word for it now, I will show you how to puzzle through finding commands and thinking about what command to use when in this book, so fret not. The command we want to use is

```
Get-EventLog -LogName Security -Newest 10
```

Take that command and start typing it into the scripting pane of the ISE, but as you go, keep hitting Tab. As you hit Tab, you will see a list of appropriate choices to type in each place of the command. For instance, as you type LogName, you will see the other parameters you can enter come up. As you type Security and hit Tab, you will see a list of event logs from which you can choose. This sort of visual representation of the universe of PowerShell, but put into a really context specific perspective, can be invaluable as you are learning PowerShell and getting your head around it.

The scripting pane is also really useful because you can use it as a kind of notepad or staging area. You can use the scripting pane to write a script or store a couple of commands, and then to test it out, you can select a part of what you have typed into the scripting pane and run only that. You do this by hitting F8 on your keyboard, or choosing the icon in the toolbar that has the green right arrow with the document image behind it. Hover over that icon to make sure you are choosing the right one. That selection will run via the PowerShell engine in the console window below (again, the blue area by default), and it is a great way to interactively build a script over time.

Believe it or not, a unique feature of the ISE is that it supports copy and paste with the same keyboard shortcuts you have been using for years. Plus, you can copy and paste not only from the scripting pane, but also from the console window, too, which unless you are running Windows 10 is kind of a difficult thing to do. You would think that since Windows has been around for 30 years that Microsoft would have figured out how to make that work, but you would be wrong.

Getting the ISE Set Up

Frankly, I think the ISE looks pretty good out of the box. There is not a lot I would recommend that you change, but you might want to adjust the font sizes for both the scripting pane and the console pane if your eyes are getting old and tired like mine. This is fairly easy to do: just go to the Tools menu and select Options, and you'll get a window like the one in Figure 1.4, where you can adjust the font, size, and color of just about every aspect of the ISE. Play around until you find something you are comfortable with and that you can read easily. This last point is important because in PowerShell, syntax is absolutely critical, and sometimes single and double quotes and tildes mean different things. You must be able to easily see the differences in characters, or you will spend hours scratching your head and troubleshooting when things go haywire.

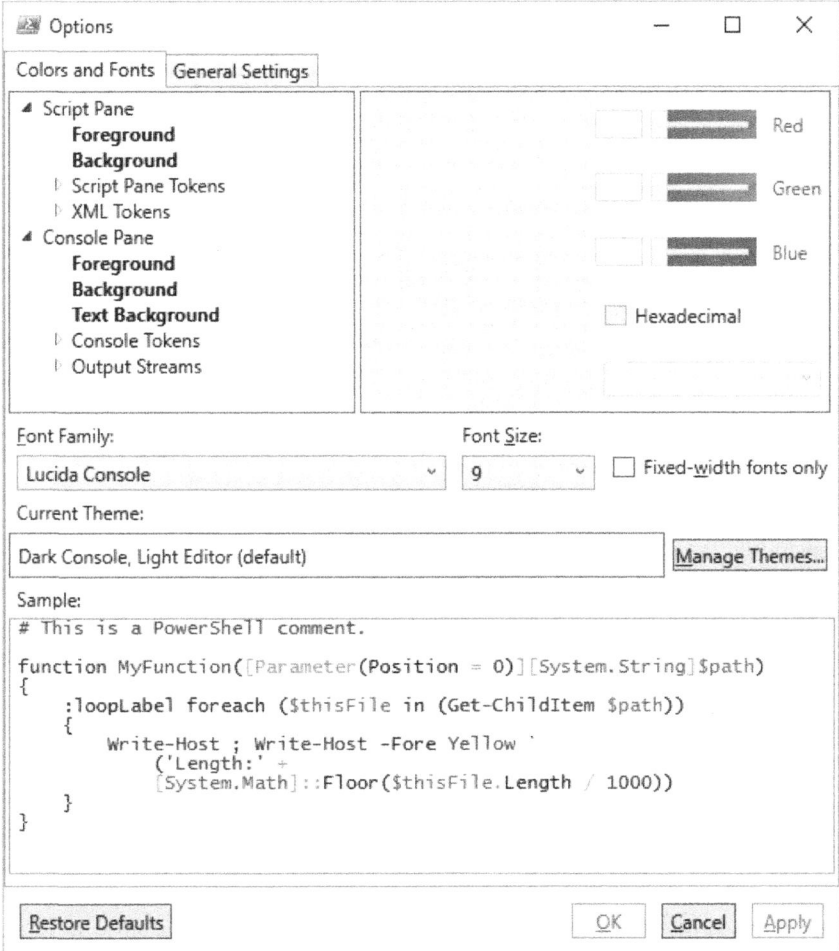

Figure 1.4: Adjusting the aesthetics of the Windows PowerShell ISE.

If you don't care about any of the colors but you just want to make things bigger, you can do that with the zoom slider in the lower right corner. This is what I do. 185% works for me. You can see this in Figure 1-.5

Figure 1.5: The Zoom slider in the lower right corner of the Windows PowerShell ISE window at 185%.

The Windows PowerShell Console

If the PowerShell ISE is the friendly neighborhood bar and grill, the PowerShell console is the median of a freeway. You had better know what you are doing, or you will get steamrolled by something moving 70 miles per hour. Well, that is not entirely true, because traffic is universally horrible everywhere (OK, so maybe that part is not true, either), but the PowerShell console is definitely where you go to get business done with no frills. It is a place where you should know what you are doing.

The PowerShell console is also generally installed on all machines that have PowerShell installed. The ISE can sometimes be missing from systems, particularly on servers that do not really have a lot of users log on to their desktops and work on them directly, but you can always rely on the console being present when you need it. It is also the easiest way to simply bang out a bunch of commands and then move on, so if you know what you want to run but you do not have those commands enclosed in a script yet, then the PowerShell console is the place you will execute those.

As I mentioned, the console is totally no frills. You can cut and paste, but only with some weird keystrokes and frankly they do not always work. The Paste most often works via a right mouse button click when you have already cut a command from another place like a text file. The cut and copy from within the console are difficult and frankly do not always work. I don't know why this is. It's frustrating, although Windows 10 seems to have improved on this somewhat. You also do not get IntelliSense, but the console does support using Tab to get some hints and suggestions for commands and the "potatoes" after the command. The difference in the console is that those suggestions do not pop up as a little graphical context menu; instead, they appear already typed out in the command line and you need to hit Tab to keep cycling through until you hit the one you want. You can also use the Shift key and hold down Tab to cycle through in the opposite direction, so if you pass a selection because you were cycling too fast, you do not have to go around the whole "wheel" of selections again.

Running the Console as an Administrator

The first thing we should talk about is security. Cue the collective groaning; security sucks. I get it. But it is important to understand that PowerShell respects your system's security and integrity, in particular because now that almost every administrative function within Windows is accessible via a PowerShell cmdlet, you can really make irreversible changes to your system with just a couple of commands. (If you want to see what I mean, take a system that you do not care about, open the PowerShell command prompt, and then type in `Get-Process | Stop-Process` and count the number of seconds it takes before you see that lovely blue screen of death.) For this reason, PowerShell limits the number of system modifying things you can do as a normal user. To get access to the really powerful stuff, you need to run as an administrator.

This is easy to do. From the Start menu, type in PowerShell, and then right-click on the item that appears and select Run as administrator. You might be prompted to enter a password, depending on how your computer's security is set up and whether you are connected to an Active Directory domain at work or you're using your home computer, or you might not. Either way you will see PowerShell running as an administrator after you satisfy the prompt for credentials. You can tell you have successfully run the PowerShell console as an administrator by looking at the title bar for the application; it will say Administrator to show you are running with what the security professionals call "elevated privilege." You can see what I mean in Figure 1.6.

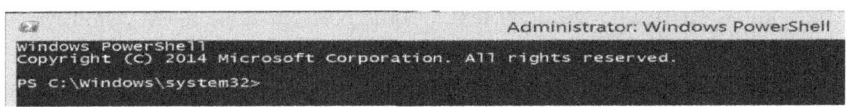

Figure 1.6: Running the Windows PowerShell console with administrative privileges.

I'll be honest with you: I'm of a mixed opinion about running PowerShell as an administrator. For instance, it's more convenient when you are learning PowerShell and its associated syntax because you have to worry only about structuring the command correctly. You don't need to spend brain cycles trying to figure out why something's working only to discover it is because of a system policy or a lack of privileges that is preventing a well structured, syntactically correct command from running. It is also more convenient to run as an administrator on a single machine. You would largely want to avoid running with elevated privileges by default if you were using the PowerShell remoting feature and trying to manage vast swaths of machines at the same time. But in a single machine and especially in a test virtual machine or a throwaway desktop without production sensitive materials on it, you will find PowerShell to be a lot less whiny about permissions errors when you run it as the king per se.

None of that is to say there are no downsides, of course. There are two sides to every coin. First of all, it is patently *insecure,* mainly because you are removing most of the built-in protections Windows has to make sure vulnerable parts of the system do not get hacked or torn apart. Second, it may be practically impossible for you to run as an administrator on your work computer simply because you may not have the credentials on your network to support this. Finally, running as an administrator does dull your awareness to which commands require privilege and which commands do not. This can sometimes lead to bad scripting and poor command structure simply because running as an administrator glosses over permissions issues, as I noted above.

I will leave it to you to decide how you want to proceed on this issue during your training, but let me be *very clear* about using PowerShell in production:

Note: Never, ever run commands as an administrator in the PowerShell console in production unless you have a very, very good reason to do so. You may break things, inadvertently repave systems, set off a nuclear war, and more.

Setting Up the Windows PowerShell Console

There are a few tweaks you can make to the console to increase visibility and make it a little more comfortable to use daily. Here are some of them.

- **Increase your command buffer.** The command buffer is basically a database or a big list held in memory of all the commands you have entered into the console during the current session; in other words, since the last time you opened the console. To access the command buffer, from the command line, just hit the up arrow and down arrow keys on your keyboard at an empty prompt to cycle through the entries in the buffer. This can be useful if you make an easy-to-fix typo in a long command, since you can just hit the up arrow to get it back and then change the error and re-run the command without having to type in the whole thing again. What I would recommend is to increase the size of this command buffer. You can do this by clicking the top left corner of the title bar, where the little icon is, selecting Properties from the pop-up context menu, and heading over to the Options tab. Take a look at Figure 1.7. Increase that buffer size to at least 100 to give you more room to maneuver, especially in long sessions where you might be troubleshooting or puzzling out a tough issue. You might need that "breadcrumb" trail.

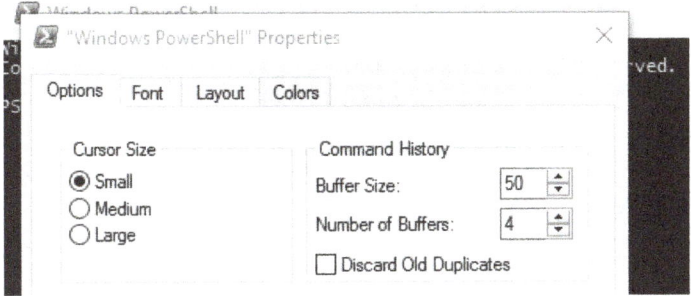

Figure 1.7: Increasing the Windows PowerShell console buffer size.

- **Change the font in the console.** A nice big font is easier on the eyes and certainly makes shorter work of finding typos. Head over to the Font tab in that same dialog (remember, click the top left corner of the title bar, where the little icon is, select Properties from the pop-up context menu, and click Fonts). I quite like Lucida Console at size 18, but my eyes are not great. Experiment to find what works for you.

- **Customize the width of the contents of the console window.** Head to the next tab, conveniently labeled Layout. Some things to change here: make the width sizes in both the screen buffer size section and the window size section the same. Figure 1.8 will show you how. This will ensure that all your text fits on screen to eliminate any scroll bars in the window. Sometimes in long commands or commands with a lot of output, some of that output prints off screen, so it's important to eliminate scroll bar if you can. It can be tough to troubleshoot commands that are not working if you can't even see the output of a command.

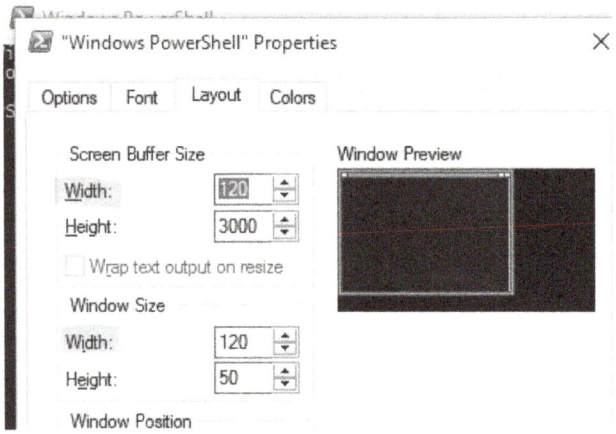

Figure 1.8: Increasing the Windows PowerShell console widths.

— **Set up high contrast colors for easier viewing.** Finally, on the Colors tab— which is the next one over—customize the colors, but make sure you choose something that contrasts well so that you don't lose track of text on the screen. For most people, the default blue background and white text works well, but for old school folks and storied administrators, a black screen with green text evokes fond memories of VAX and AS/400 machines. You choose what works for you.

Running and Stopping Commands in the Console

Once you have the console all customized to your liking, you can begin running commands. A quick tour of how this works: you type the command at the prompt, just as you would in a DOS command line environment. Hitting Enter will execute the command, just as you would expect.

Using Ctrl-C will *not* copy text as it would in Word or any other common Windows application. Instead, Ctrl-C in the PowerShell console stops the current command from running. This is most useful when you mistakenly run a command without including the right stuff after the main part of the command; PowerShell will notice the required information is missing and it will prompt you for it, and when you see this you can hit Ctrl-C to cancel out of the command and start over. This is also useful if you are reading a help page, which for some commands can stretch over 10 or 20 screens. Once you have read to the section you wanted and found the information you were looking for, you can hit Ctrl-C to "exit" the help environment (which is really stopping the Get-Help command, but more on that as we get deeper into the book) and get back to the console prompt.

Windows PowerShell Console Caveats

There is never a perfect solution for any one problem, and that maxim continues to be true with PowerShell. While sometimes a crunchy terminal window and a will-to-get-stuff-done are all you need, other times that same window will be a pit of despair, like looking over an abyss in moonlight. (The howling you hear is the simile I have just stretched into oblivion.)

First and foremost, if you are one of my international readers—hello and welcome to you! The PowerShell console is not well localized. It does not display non-English languages well at all. Second, as I discussed in the previous section, copying and pasting work is a little different in the console window. Ctrl-C, as you know now, stops a command from executing, and Ctrl-V works generally as you would expect to paste the contents of the clipboard into the prompt. However, for some reason Ctrl-V doesn't always work, so a shortcut I have found particularly useful is to use the right mouse button—just click anywhere inside the console window with the right mouse button and the contents of the clipboard will be pasted into the current prompt entry. But still, it's not as seamless as you might expect it to be.

One of the biggest differences in actually running commands one by one or in smaller batches is that the console does not include IntelliSense as the ISE does. It only allows for discovery and typing shortcuts via hitting the Tab key, known as "tab completion."

Tab Completion

"What's that about tab completion?" you say. Well, consider it to be the little brother of the IntelliSense feature in the Windows PowerShell ISE I covered in the last main section. The best way to show you is via a hands-on demonstration. Let's take a slightly different version of the command we were using earlier:

```
Get-EventLog -LogName Application -Newest 5
```

Start typing that into a fresh PowerShell console window. After you type `Get-Event`, hit Tab. You'll see PowerShell fills in the `Log` part. Then add the potatoes: type in the hyphen and then hit Tab again, and then again and again. You can see PowerShell cycling through the available choices. You can also use Shift-

Tab to go backwards in the cycle in case you're hitting the keys too quickly and miss the choice you need.

Some PowerShell users feel like this is tougher to use than the ISE when one is learning PowerShell because you don't get that pop-up window of choices in the console. Some feel like tab completion is helpful mostly only if you already have an idea about what choices are out there, kind of like the old saying about the massive IBM Redbook technical manuals, that they were "clear only if previously known." I'm not sure I agree with that, but I do see where a menu would be easier to visually grasp. But that's why you have the ISE. For those quick one or two commands, especially when you find yourself getting more adept at PowerShell syntax, the tab completion feature in the console can save you a lot of typing and potential carpal tunnel syndrome.

The Last Word

As I mentioned, my goal for this first chapter of *Learning PowerShell* was to get you set up and ready to start working. We looked at the PowerShell ISE, the PowerShell console, how to make sure you're on the right platforms to get started with PowerShell, and how to use some of the features of each of these environments to make it easier to get your work done and also to support your learning of PowerShell. In the next chapter, we'll dive into the meat of PowerShell and start learning the basics. There is, after all, no time like the present.

Chapter 2
The Basics of PowerShell

Welcome to Chapter 2 of *Learning PowerShell*. There is no avoiding it: it's time to learn PowerShell, and by this, I mean learn how it's structured and how to do some simple things. In this chapter, my main goal is to lay the foundation for PowerShell basics. This will be an important chapter, so don't feel intimidated—or ashamed if you find yourself needing to read it a few times. Nothing wrong with that! I'll hold your hand as we get started. Without further ado, let's dive in.

Some Terminology and Definitions

Before we go too far, we need to agree on a common vernacular. In PowerShell specific words mean very specific things, and sometimes you can use one word and in other times you can't use the same word. To avoid confusion I want to lay a bunch of these definitions out at the start, so we can all be on the same page. I'll start with the most important one.

- **cmdlet.** A cmdlet, which you pronounce "command-let," is a feature unique to PowerShell and represents something you would run at the command line. Cmdlets themselves are written in a language supported by the Microsoft .NET Framework, basically with C# or VB.Net. As I said, cmdlets work only in PowerShell, so if you use "cmdlet" as an additional search term on Google when searching for something, you probably will limit that search to largely PowerShell results, which is a good thing.
- **function.** A function is a cmdlet that is not written in .NET and that uses only native commands to PowerShell. Consider a function like a bunch of built-in PowerShell cmdlets strung together to achieve some objective. The main difference here is that a function is usually a container of other cmdlets, whereas a cmdlet generally does one small thing and one small thing only. You could say that a function might make a cake but a cmdlet would add the baking powder to the baking dish.
- **workflow.** A workflow is a special kind of function that executes cmdlets or other functions in a specific, defined order. Workflows are a special feature of PowerShell and need a little prewiring in order to work the first time, but they can be very powerful at firing off cmdlets based on certain events happening or not happening and ultimately achieving some known end state.

DOI 10.1515/9781501506673-002

- **command.** A command is sort of shorthand for cmdlet, function, or work-flow. You can use it fairly interchangeably and it helps when you are speaking with folks who are not as invested in PowerShell and who don't concern themselves with the nuances of the language.
- **alias.** An alias is a short name for command. This deserves some further explanation, which I'll do in the next section.

A Little about Aliases

An alias, as I mentioned, is basically a shorter name for a command, like a nickname. Essentially the only idea behind an alias is to save you some typing, since some command names are really long. These aliases exist just to save you some typing and enable that lazy side that we all have. After all, who wants to type Format-Table when we can just say ft instead?

And, yes, ft is a real alias that works everywhere. In fact, there are a lot of aliases (on your system already). From the PowerShell console, use Get-Alias for a complete list of pre-existing aliases on your system. For easy reference, I'll include the ones that are installed and set up by default on the Windows 10-based system I am using to write this book.

```
% -> ForEach-Object
? -> Where-Object
ac -> Add-Content
asnp -> Add-PSSnapin
cat -> Get-Content
cd -> Set-Location
CFS -> ConvertFrom-String
chdir -> Set-Location
clc -> Clear-Content
clear -> Clear-Host
clhy -> Clear-History
cli -> Clear-Item
clp -> Clear-ItemProperty
cls -> Clear-Host
clv -> Clear-Variable
cnsn -> Connect-PSSession
compare -> Compare-Object
copy -> Copy-Item
cp -> Copy-Item
cpi -> Copy-Item
cpp -> Copy-ItemProperty
```

```
curl -> Invoke-WebRequest
cvpa -> Convert-Path
dbp -> Disable-PSBreakpoint
del -> Remove-Item
diff -> Compare-Object
dir -> Get-ChildItem
dnsn -> Disconnect-PSSession
ebp -> Enable-PSBreakpoint
echo -> Write-Output
epcsv -> Export-Csv
epsn -> Export-PSSession
erase -> Remove-Item
etsn -> Enter-PSSession
exsn -> Exit-PSSession
fc -> Format-Custom
fhx -> Format-Hex
fl -> Format-List
foreach -> ForEach-Object
ft -> Format-Table
fw -> Format-Wide
gbp -> Get-PSBreakpoint
gc -> Get-Content
gcb -> Get-Clipboard
gci -> Get-ChildItem
gcm -> Get-Command
gcs -> Get-PSCallStack
gdr -> Get-PSDrive
ghy -> Get-History
gi -> Get-Item
gjb -> Get-Job
gl -> Get-Location
gm -> Get-Member
gmo -> Get-Module
gp -> Get-ItemProperty
gps -> Get-Process
gpv -> Get-ItemPropertyValue
group -> Group-Object
gsn -> Get-PSSession
gsnp -> Get-PSSnapin
gsv -> Get-Service
gu -> Get-Unique
gv -> Get-Variable
gwmi -> Get-WmiObject
h -> Get-History
history -> Get-History
```

```
icm -> Invoke-Command
iex -> Invoke-Expression
ihy -> Invoke-History
ii -> Invoke-Item
ipcsv -> Import-Csv
ipmo -> Import-Module
ipsn -> Import-PSSession
irm -> Invoke-RestMethod
ise -> powershell_ise.exe
iwmi -> Invoke-WmiMethod
iwr -> Invoke-WebRequest
kill -> Stop-Process
lp -> Out-Printer
ls -> Get-ChildItem
man -> help
md -> mkdir
measure -> Measure-Object
mi -> Move-Item
mount -> New-PSDrive
move -> Move-Item
mp -> Move-ItemProperty
mv -> Move-Item
ndr -> New-PSDrive
ni -> New-Item
nmo -> New-Module
npssc -> New-PSSessionConfigurationFile
nsn -> New-PSSession
nv -> New-Variable
ogv -> Out-GridView
oh -> Out-Host
popd -> Pop-Location
ps -> Get-Process
pushd -> Push-Location
pwd -> Get-Location
r -> Invoke-History
rbp -> Remove-PSBreakpoint
rcjb -> Receive-Job
rcsn -> Receive-PSSession
rd -> Remove-Item
rdr -> Remove-PSDrive
ren -> Rename-Item
ri -> Remove-Item
rjb -> Remove-Job
rm -> Remove-Item
rmdir -> Remove-Item
```

```
rmo -> Remove-Module
rni -> Rename-Item
rnp -> Rename-ItemProperty
rp -> Remove-ItemProperty
rsn -> Remove-PSSession
rsnp -> Remove-PSSnapin
rujb -> Resume-Job
rv -> Remove-Variable
rvpa -> Resolve-Path
rwmi -> Remove-WmiObject
sajb -> Start-Job
saps -> Start-Process
sasv -> Start-Service
sbp -> Set-PSBreakpoint
sc -> Set-Content
scb -> Set-Clipboard
select -> Select-Object
set -> Set-Variable
shcm -> Show-Command
si -> Set-Item
sl -> Set-Location
sleep -> Start-Sleep
sls -> Select-String
sort -> Sort-Object
sp -> Set-ItemProperty
spjb -> Stop-Job
spps -> Stop-Process
spsv -> Stop-Service
start -> Start-Process
sujb -> Suspend-Job
sv -> Set-Variable
swmi -> Set-WmiInstance
tee -> Tee-Object
trcm -> Trace-Command
type -> Get-Content
wget -> Invoke-WebRequest
where -> Where-Object
wjb -> Wait-Job
write -> Write-Output
```

Sometimes when you are Googling or Binging for help with a PowerShell command, you might see others on the Internet using aliases you don't understand. Fret not because it is easy to decode these aliases. Simply use

```
get-help alias
```

And replace alias with the alias in question. For example, using my previous example of `ft`, if I wanted to decode that, I'd use

```
get-help ft
```

And I would get back what we see in Figure 2.1.

```
PS C:\Users\Jon> get-help ft
NAME
    Format-Table
SYNTAX
    Format-Table [[-Property] <Object[]>] [-AutoSize] [-HideTableHeaders] [-Wrap] [-GroupBy <Object>] [-View <string>]
    [-ShowError] [-DisplayError] [-Force] [-Expand <string> {CoreOnly | EnumOnly | Both}] [-InputObject <psobject>]
    [<CommonParameters>]


ALIASES
    ft


REMARKS
    Get-Help cannot find the Help files for this cmdlet on this computer. It is displaying only partial help.
        -- To download and install Help files for the module that includes this cmdlet, use Update-Help.
        -- To view the Help topic for this cmdlet online, type: "Get-Help Format-Table -Online" or
           go to http://go.microsoft.com/fwlink/?LinkID=113303.
```

Figure 2.1: Decoding an alias using the get-help command.

Astute readers might be asking if you can create your own alias for commands or functions not already installed out of the box. The answer is yes, you can, but doing so is not terribly useful. Why? Mainly because aliases do not survive your closing the console window unless you specifically export them and then reimport them when you re-open the console window. You'd have to do this each and every time for the aliases to stay persistent. Plus, that works only on one machine. Your aliases would not be configured on other systems unless you do the export/import routine on those systems, too. Further, they can muddy the waters of scripts and functions you write, especially if you create the aliases for really outlandish, rarely used commands and then leave for months before coming back to your script. You could really scratch your head and ask what in the world you were trying to do. For these reasons, I recommend you stick to the set of common pre-installed aliases that I listed above for you. PowerShell is hard enough to parse for a newbie that adding aliases as a compounding factor really does not save you any time.

Good news! That's all the terminology we have to worry about right now. Let's move on.

PowerShell Command Components

PowerShell has a specific syntax that you need to use when you're working with the language. The syntax is what makes some PowerShell code look like Greek, but that's only because the syntax is the way we translate what we are thinking objective-wise into language the computer can understand. That syntax for a basic command is

```
Verb-Noun -parameter value -anotherparameter anothervalue -switch
```

Don't worry, I'm going to dive into each of these things, starting now.

Commands

PowerShell is, at its core, a bunch of commands. You can combine them, pipe them, connect them, filter their output, sort their output, do all sorts of handstands and dances with them, but ultimately PowerShell is commands. So it behooves us to learn the basic structure of a command, and luckily PowerShell follows a consistent format in naming its commands. This basic format, or syntax, is

```
Verb-Noun
```

Think back to some of the examples I used in Chapter 1.

```
Get-EventLog
Format-Table
Get-Process
Stop-Process
```

See the verbs? `Get`, `Format`, `Stop`—they're all verbs. And the nouns? `EventLog`, `Table`, `Process`. All PowerShell commands work this way. They do *an action* to *something*. In Chapter 1, I called this the meat of PowerShell, the big part without which none of the rest of the stuff matters.

Parameters

But what about the potatoes? Those potatoes are called *parameters*, and I like to think of parameters as where the wheeling and dealing in PowerShell gets done.

If the command is Verb-Noun and tells the future, the parameters tell the specific things about the future that we care about.

As it happens, there are actually several types of parameters.

- There are single-value parameters, like -Newest 5. The parameter name is -Newest and the value is 5.
- There are multi-value parameters, like -Extensions '.ade,.adp, .app,.asp' and in these situations, you can see the values are separated by commas with no spaces. There are also quote marks, and these are sometimes necessary and at other times they are not. Stay with me; I'll talk about the quote marks in a minute.
- There are switches, which are basically like light switches in that they have two possible values, on and off. Practically speaking, switch parameters (which we shorten to switches because, well, I'm lazy) are always assumed to be off unless you include them in the parameter set for a command, and if you include them, they're assumed to be on. So in neither case do you need to add a value. For example, in the Verb-Noun -Verbose command, which is not real by the way, the switch is -Verbose and it doesn't have a value.

Syntax

There is some ticky tacky stuff that goes along with this. Parameters must start with a hyphen (–) and then immediately start the text of the parameter name, with no space. This often trips up newbies who think – Newest 5 will work. It won't. -Newest 5 is the way to go, with no space between the hyphen and "newest." Then, there is a space after the end of the parameter name and before the value. There is also a space between one parameter value and the hyphen that precedes the next parameter name. Take a look:

```
Get-EventLog -LogName Application -Newest 5
```

See that there:

- are no spaces between the hyphens that precede the parameter name
- are spaces between the parameter name and its value
- are spaces between the first value and the hyphen preceding the second parameter name

Also, all of this is case insensitive. PowerShell doesn't care about capital letters, lowercase letters, cAmElCaSe words, and so on. So spend your time making sure your spaces and hyphens are right.

Now, about those pesky quote marks. In multi-value parameters, the ones that are separated with single commas and no spaces, you might need to include quote marks. While you can use double quote marks (for example, "), I recommend single quote marks (') for the avoidance of doubt. When do you need to use these quote marks? Basically, if there are spaces or other punctuation, you need quote marks. If there are no spaces or no other punctuation, then you can leave them out.

Let's use directory names as an example. If we were specifying directory names in a multi-value parameter, we would need to enclose these directory names in single quote marks because the long file names include spaces. So we would use single quote marks around the directory name and put the commas that separate the multiple values outside of the quote marks, like this:

```
'C:\Program Files','D:\Users','E:\FileFolderFullOfKidPhotos'
```

needed

But if I'm just specifying numbers in a multi-value parameters, since there are no spaces or punctuation, I don't need to bother with quotes.

```
1,2,45398475,234987
```

← _not needed_

It's really the spaces that trip people up. Basically, if there is a space in something you are giving to PowerShell, you will need to "treat" it with quote marks. This is known in coding parlance as "escaping" the text so that spaces are treated as part of what you're giving PowerShell and not as part of the syntax of a command PowerShell should know—that is where it gets confused.

Types of Parameter Values

Those parameter values can come in a lot of different forms, and you will see some of these called out sometimes.

Strings. Strings are just letters and numbers, and this follows the same rule as we just learned: if your string includes spaces, then the whole string has to be enclosed in quotes. Strings are primarily text and numbers that should be treated as text, like labels and messages to display (and not parts of an equation to do math to, for example).

`Int, Int32, Int64`. These are all pretty much the same way to say a whole number, or a round number, with no decimal. 3, not 2.5. 983, not 983.2.

`DateTime`. This is simply a month, day, and year, like $10-21-2015$.

Arrays, collections, and lists. These are basically all ways of saying multiple values are OK for something, but they are all different ways of organizing those multiple values. The syntax for arrays, collections, and lists uses the [] characters, as in `<myfamily[son,daughter,wife,mother,father]>`. As you saw, commas are used to separate the individual values, and—you guessed it—any individual value in a list with spaces needs quote marks. You don't use quote marks over the whole list, again, but only surrounding the individual values; leave the commas unenclosed by quotes. When you're running directly from the command line and you don't specify values before hitting Enter, PowerShell will prompt you to enter the values as a list, one at a time, hitting Enter after each. If you encounter this, you may wonder how to stop entering values. It's easy: when you're done, just hit Enter on a blank line, and processing of the command will continue now that you have given all of the required input.

Some Parameters are Positional Parameters

Positional parameters are parameters that are used pretty often and used consistently in the same ways, enough so that PowerShell can puzzle out what values mean without requiring you to type the names of the parameter. These positional parameters require values to be in certain positions in the command syntax, and the upshot is that you don't have to type the name of the parameter, just the value, because PowerShell knows the name by virtue of the position.

For example, in our commonly used `Get-EventLog` example, the `-LogName` parameter is actually positional. We don't have to type in `-LogName` because PowerShell knows that the first thing after the command itself should be the name of the log we care about. So I can just do

```
Get-EventLog Application -Newest 5
```

And it works just fine.

Now, not all parameters are positional. If you use positional parameters and leave out the parameter names when you are writing your commands, you must put the positional (nameless) parameters in the right places before any non-positional parameters are used. Alternatively, you can just include the name of a positional parameter as we've been doing all along, and when you do that, you can put it anywhere, because the order—the position—only matters when you omit the name and rely on the position.

Optional Parameters

Almost every cmdlet has one optional parameter. You'll learn how to tell all of these apart later in this chapter when we talk about how to get help from within PowerShell. But suffice it to say you will hardly ever use all of the parameters any given individual command supports. If you don't need the parameters, you can simply exclude them. You don't need to enter them and leave them empty. Just ignore them.

Mandatory Parameters

Mandatory errors are exactly what they sound like. If you leave mandatory parameters out, PowerShell will throw up errors. In some cases PowerShell will prompt you for their values when you run the cmdlets in the console interactively, as I discussed in the arrays, collections, and lists bullet point earlier in this chapter.

Parameter Sets – The Fork in The Road

Some commands do a lot. Sometimes, they do so much that they need two different sets of parameters, each with different allowable, mandatory, and optional parameters: one that has to do with some subaction, and another that relates to yet another subaction. These are parameter sets, and they are like a fork in the road: once you use a parameter out of one set, you can't use one out of another set in the same command. Sometimes parameters are shared between multiple sets and these are OK, but non-shared parameters operate under the rule of " pick one and go with it," and no switching is allowed. (Don't worry too much about this yet, but I wanted to let you know that this exists as you will see a couple of examples later in this chapter of commands with parameter sets.)

Common Parameters

There are a set of common parameters that all cmdlets in PowerShell support. These are as follows.

- `-Verbose`. Shows information in volume about what's going on. This is useful for troubleshooting.
- `-Debug`. Shows stuff of interest to developers.
- `-WarningAction`. Tells PowerShell what to do upon a recoverable warning. There are four choices: `Continue`, `Inquire`, `Silentlycontinue`, and `stop`.
- `-WarningVariable`. Stores the warnings any given command displays when it is run in a variable you can get later.

- `-ErrorAction`. For errors you can recover from, you can choose what to do while the command is running: `Continue`, `Ignore`, `Inquire`, `Silentlycontinue`, `stop`, and `suspend`.
- `-ErrorVariable`. Stores errors in a placeholder you can query later.
- `-OutVariable`. Stores output in a variable you can grab later.
- `-OutBuffer`. Shows how many things can queue up before being written to the pipeline (for advanced users).
- `-WhatIf`. This is a super useful common parameter because it shows what the result of the command would be if you ran it. It is a great way to avoid a huge and costly mistake.
- `-Confirm`. Prompts you for a final yes or no before executing a command.

Shortcuts

Ah, shortcuts, or as I like to call them, music to the ears of lazy administrators everywhere. I can say that because I *am* one, and I *have been* there. I know what it's like. In PowerShell, there are numerous shortcuts you can learn to use throughout the language. Right now there are a couple that make sense for you as a beginner.

Again, you can use aliases, as we discussed above. These are most useful for those built-in common cmdlets that will be the same on every system you touch. You may be surprised to learn that some parameter names also have aliases but you'll be hard pressed to find them yourself; most come from experience. You'll see them during your daily work, some will stand out, a few you'll actually remember, and even fewer will make it into your scripts, but that is the nature of the game. Nothing wrong with using those.

You also can truncate things. Parameter names can be truncated as long as you type enough of the parameter to make it uniquely identifiable when PowerShell is running the command. Returning to our often used `Get-EventLog` example, the following works just fine and I've saved myself a few keystrokes:

```
Get-EventLog -LogN Application -Ne 5
```

See that I left off "ame" from `-LogName` and "west" from `-Newest` and the command still ran. You'll have to play around with this a little as sometimes there are multiple parameter names that have a lot of letters in common, and in those situations this is much less useful as a shortcut. But sometimes it will save you some effort.

External Commands

Inside the PowerShell console are access to common DOS command-line functions you might already be familiar with—like `dir`, `ping`, `net use x: \\UNC\path` to map a drive, and `tracert` to figure out where some network function is failing. These typical utilties are executed by PowerShell right from within the window, allowing you to mix and match your scripting goodness with falling back on some old-school DOS hackery at the same time. This is nice, but sometimes especially with some less common DOS command, PowerShell simply does not understand them and so attempts to parse them like a PowerShell command, where you need hyphens and single quotes and parameters and all that jazz. This can result in DOS commands failing and a lot of unexpected problems if you do not understand and recognize what is going on.

Fear not, however, as there is an easy solution to this issue. When you're running any DOS command, simply stick two hyphen characters (--) after the name of the external command, and PowerShell will just get out of the way. It will not try to parse or interpret the statement and will instead launch CMD, the built-in Windows native command prompt, and run the command there instead and then pipe the output right back to your window. Of course, this maneuver isn't always required, especially with those common DOS commands I outlined above, but it is actually a good habit to acquire when you are mixing external commands with PowerShell.

Commands Within Commands

Part of the power of PowerShell is the ability to nest things—functions within functions, commands within commands, and in general to be able to do more than one command at a time. This is where the really interesting scripting and the really productive work actually gets done. Let me introduce you now to the ability of PowerShell to put a command within another command.

Nesting commands like this is useful for commands with parameters that accept lists of values. If you remember back to middle school math, you might remember the order of operations in arithmetic, which basically is: everything in parenthesis, then multiplication, then division, then addition, then subtraction, from left to right. Burying commands in PowerShell works similarly in that you use parenthesis ( ) to encapsulate the command in any given statement that PowerShell should execute first.

Let's use `Get-Content` as a pretty useful example here. What we want to do is have a list of computers in a text file, and then we want to see the processes that are running on each of those computers. First we need to read that file in, and then use the contents of the file to "fuel" the `Get-Process` command. The

`Get-Content` command is great for reading in information that is stored in a file. So to put this together, let's assume our list of computers we care about is stored in a file called `list.txt`. To read that file in, we would use

```
Get-Content list.txt
```

That's going to read the file. Then we need the other part of the puzzle: how do we use `Get-Process`? To run it on a computer called COMPUTER we would use:

```
Get-Process -Computer COMPUTER
```

But in this case, instead of COMPUTER we want the names of the systems in that file. All we have to do is put the commands together.

```
Get-Process -Computer (Get-Content list.txt)
```

Since the command in parenthesis is executed first, we're reading in the names from the file and then those names are used by PowerShell for the Get-Process command. Can you think of any other places this might be helpful? What about:

— reading a list of mailboxes to create and then using an Exchange PowerShell command to create those mailboxes?
— reading a list of usernames that your human resources department provides to then reassign to a different group within Active Directory consequent to a corporate reorganization?
— and many more.

So that's PowerShell commands at their most fundamental. Now let's see how you figure out which commands to use when and how to use their associated parameters to get what you want done.

Knowing Which Commands to Use and How to Use Them: Getting Help

Repeat after me: the Help files are the single best resource you will find as a user of PowerShell. The Help files built into PowerShell are almost universal, they are right at your fingertips, and they offer the least friction when it comes to getting immediate information about what commands are available and how to use those commands.

Now this is not to say that the help files are perfect. They are sometimes in-complete, especially for newer commands or commands added by other software or third-party vendors. They are not always correct, although they mostly are. And sometimes they are written in that sort of technical speak that will just make you scratch your head and wonder why. But make no mistake: *the help files should be your primary resource when you have a question about a PowerShell com-mand either being available or its associated syntax.* Google and Bing are great for ideas but they should be used only after you've looked at the help, tried to under-stand what the help file says, and then have come up short in your search for information.

The Help files are extremely useful and always available precisely because they have been designed to be updated on the fly. Microsoft and other PowerShell command module makers can always include updateable help, so as support cases and other popular uses of the command make certain issues clear, those can be documented within the help files and made available to other users. You can always get the latest help for your particular configuration of PowerShell by running `update-help` as an administrator. You may want to schedule a re-minder to run this command monthly so that you're always working from the freshest copy of help files.

Let's consider using help from a couple of different perspectives: from one standpoint, when you know the command you want to use, but aren't sure of its supported parameters or the syntax required to use it; and from the other stand-point, when you simply have an idea or a concept or a general task to get done, but you do not know any specific commands to carry you forward.

Looking at Help for a Known Command

When you know the command you want to use but you need some guidance about exactly *how* to use it, then you can use `get-help command | more` to get all of the details. For example, with our `Get-Content` example from above, here's what I would type in

```
Get-Help Get-Content | more
```

That would result in the following output in the console, as shown in Figure 2.2:

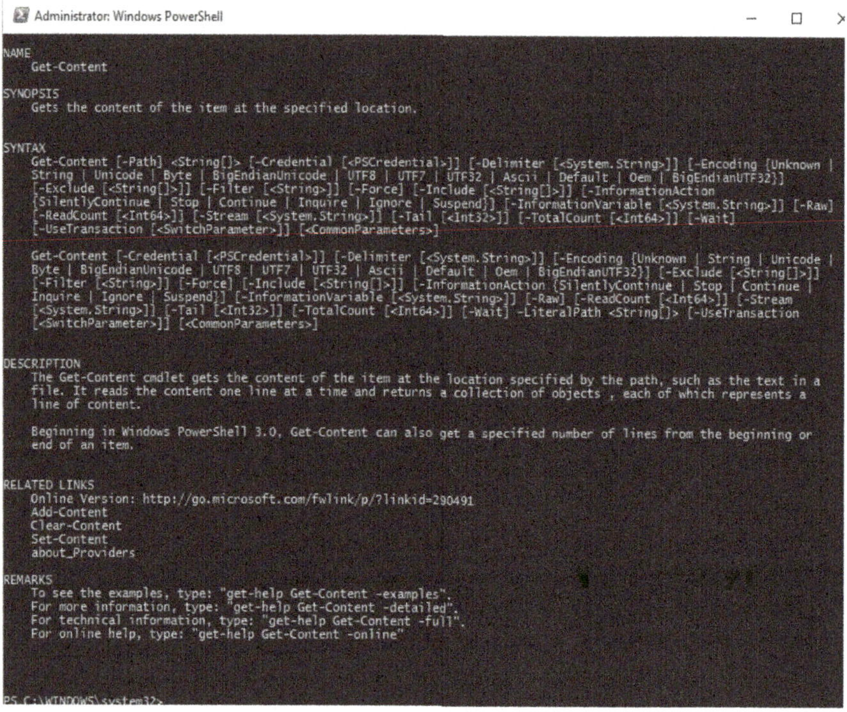

Figure 2. 2: Using the Get-Help command for a specific, known command

- To save yourself some keystrokes, you can always use `help`, which is an alias for Get-Help and will mean the same thing.
- So how do you decode the output of the help command? The most obvious part is the listing of parameters and their required syntax. Specifically:
- The [and] surrounding some parameters means that those parameters are optional—as we discussed, you can ignore these if you don't need them.
- Positional parameters will show only the parameter name in [and] –the value will have nothing around it, so that is how you tell which parameter is positional.
- Switches are denoted as [<SwitchParameter>]. When you read this, an easy rule of thumb is to leave it out or leave it blank: it's an on/off light switch vs. a game of mad libs, so it doesn't have a value. Its presence means the switch is on; its absence means the switch is off.

Using Get-Help will also sometimes show some examples of the command in use at the bottom of help screens. The presence of examples can vary, depending on the command, but if there are any examples available, you can simply add the example parameter to `Get-Help` to see them. For example, to see the examples for the `Get-Mailbox` command, you would use

```
get-help get-mailbox -example
```

Looking for Help With an Idea or Concept

Much more common at least in the beginning stages of using and learning PowerShell is the sense that, "yeah, I'd like to be able to do stuff surrounding, say, event logs" but you don't know right off the top of your head the PowerShell commands that would work for that general subject. And that might not ever fully come for you, given that there are, at least on my system, 1,448 commands installed by default. That's without adding Exchange or SharePoint commands or even running this on a Windows Server machine, where there are even more commands that ship in the box.

Suffice it to say, you're going to want a catalog of commands at your fingertips for pretty much the first year of working with PowerShell, and even longer than that in some cases. Fortunately, PowerShell ships with a powerful search function that lets you use wildcards in the help system to look for commands dealing with certain nouns. The most common search is using the asterisk wildcard (*) and using that wildcard both in front of and behind the noun for which you are searching for related commands. For example:

```
Get-Help *security*
```

```
Help *mailbox*
```

Both of those commands will put out a list of related commands that can be used. This is the primary way of finding out what commands relate to a given theme or concept.

Full, Unrestrained, Painstakingly Detailed Help

The help files available in Windows PowerShell have two lengths: the summary or truncated version, which is shown through the standard `Get-Help` command, and the full, detailed help, which shows when you use the `-full` switch on the Get-Help command. This shows *a lot* more information, including:

— the parameter name and value
— a description of the parameter
— whether that parameter is required
— the positional nature of the parameter (either "yes, this is a positional parameter" and then the position number of the parameter, or it's not positional and simply a named parameter)
— the parameter's default value
— whether it takes the pipeline input (more about the pipeline in a later chapter)
— whether you can use a wildcard or not

Sometimes the full help is a little too detailed and can be overwhelming, which was generally Microsoft's idea behind making the summary help the displayed default help. But always know that if you need to do a little more digging into any given command, you can do so via the `-full` parameter.

A Little Interactive Handholding: `Show-Command`

Sometimes the command line and the console can be a little daunting, especially with a relatively complex command with a lot of parameters that must be sequentially presented. Throw in a pair of not-so-good eyes and you can waste a lot of time searching for a stray space or a parameter in the wrong position.

Enter `Show-Commmand` which pops up a GUI dialog box to help you complete a command. This feature is really useful if you forget syntax or need to learn how a command works. You just call it by saying `Show-Command` and then the name of the command you need help using:

```
Show-Command Get-EventLog
```

This pops up the dialog box shown in Figure 2.3.

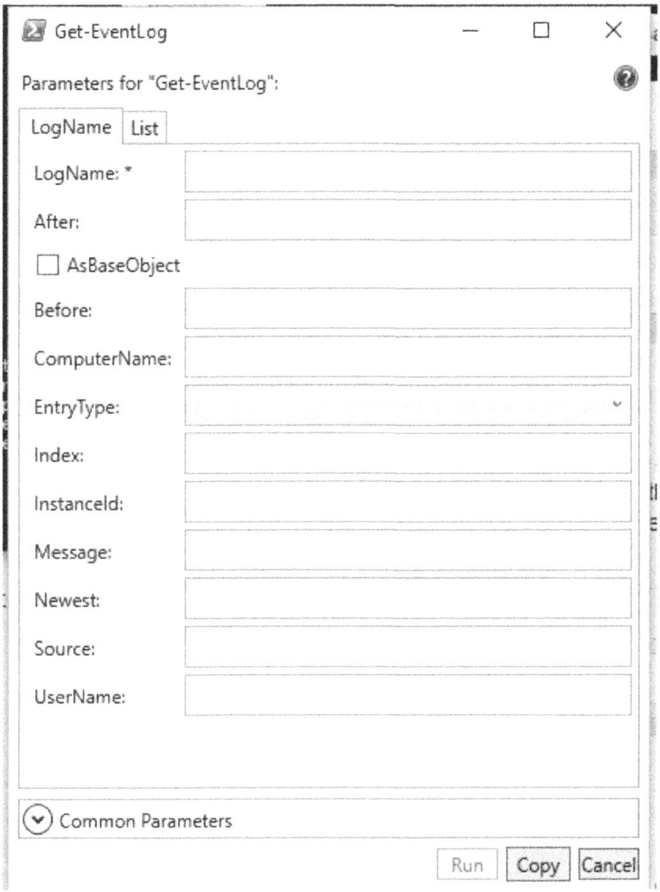

Figure 2.3: Using the `Show-Command` command to get a little extra hand-holding when using new-to-you commands.

The box shows you all the parameters you can use with the command. Again, you can leave out the optional parameters. The tool takes care of positional parameters and makes sure the syntax is correct. You just pop in the required parameters, which are denoted with the asterisk, and then either click Run at the bottom to execute the command immediately within the console, or click the Copy button to copy the command to the clipboard and then from there you can paste the resulting well formed command into the console. You can also use this tool with the Windows PowerShell Integrated Scripting Environment, or ISE, that I covered in Chapter 1.

One caveat for the Show-Command tool: it works only with single commands. If you need to form multiple commands and nest them, use the Copy function to copy to a separate area and form the overarching command there.

Understanding Error Messages

For a PowerShell beginner, you're going to do a lot of things wrong. Hell, I consider myself an intermediate user of PowerShell and yet I still do a lot of things wrong. The red error messages you get from PowerShell seem cold and unfriendly and are sometimes difficult to parse. But they do contain key information that could help you figure out why PowerShell isn't doing what you're telling it to do, and how to fix it.

Let's look at a sample error message, shown in Figure 2.4.

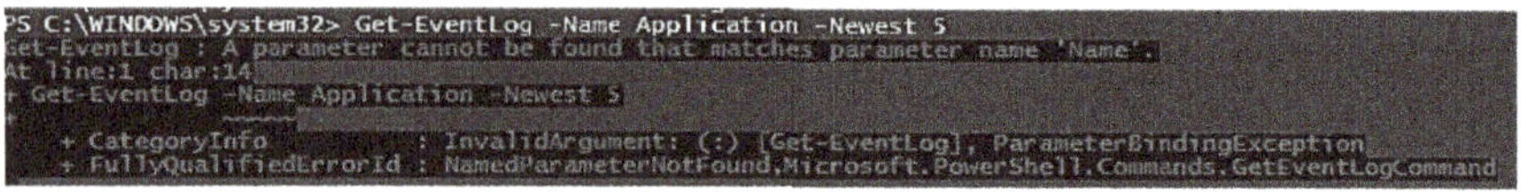

```
PS C:\WINDOWS\system32> Get-EventLog -Name Application -Newest 5
Get-EventLog : A parameter cannot be found that matches parameter name 'Name'.
At line:1 char:14
+ Get-EventLog -Name Application -Newest 5
    + CategoryInfo          : InvalidArgument: (:) [Get-EventLog], ParameterBindingException
    + FullyQualifiedErrorId : NamedParameterNotFound,Microsoft.PowerShell.Commands.GetEventLogCommand
```

Figure 2.4: Deciphering a PowerShell error message.

In this case, the error is reasonably clear: "A parameter cannot be found that matches parameter name 'Name'" is a tortured way of saying that "Name" is not a valid parameter. You will notice that this overly long and hard-to-decipher way of spitting out error messages is, regrettably, fairly prevalent in PowerShell. It sure doesn't help newbies get along with the language and I am sure there is some arcane technical reason for error messages being worded in this style, but I sure don't think it is super helpful. In any case, sometimes those statements are actually so unclear as to be unhelpful. The real meat of the information is on the next line, where it says a line number and a "char" number, which means the character number. In this case, on line 1 (which is expected since my command was only one line long) and at character position 14 (so put the cursor at the beginning of the command and then count over 14 letters, including spaces) we see the problem: "Name" isn't actually a parameter.

Often you will need to *read the help* when you get error messages like this. But knowing the line and character position of the error will help narrow down where you should start your troubleshooting. And if you keep getting errors like this, don't be afraid to use Show-Command and compare what it spits out with what you were trying to type; lots of on-the-fly education happens this way, and it is nothing to be ashamed of. Trial by fire is a big part of how *everyone* learns PowerShell, and do not let anyone tell you otherwise.

Always Use Protection: Stopping You from Hurting Yourself

PowerShell has the concept of an *impact level*, which is an internally defined level that shows how much of an impact to the local system that running a command can have. After all, some commands—mostly the `Get-*` commands that only retrieve information—don't do any altering of the system, but some other commands that have an action to them can irreparably harm a system. PowerShell understands the differences in these commands and assigns an impact level to most commands. It also sets an impact level threshold, which prompts PowerShell to ask you to verify before executing a command that you in fact really want that command to execute; you get that prompt if the impact level of a command is equal to or higher than that threshold, and you are not prompted at all if the command's impact level is lower than the threshold.

You can check the value of that threshold by typing in `$confirmpreference` at the command line. On mine, this reports back `High`, and this means if I run any command with an impact level of high, I'll get a prompt that in fact is like running the `confirm` switch after a command, one of the common operators we talked about earlier in this chapter. But that's why sometimes if you are using sensitive commands, you will get a prompt that you otherwise do not get.

The Last Word

As I mentioned, my goal for this second chapter of *Learning PowerShell* was to get you familiar with the basics of a command and its parameters. That, at its core, is what PowerShell is. I took you through commands, parameters, how they work, what they include, and the different types of parameters you will come across as you work with PowerShell. I also introduced the help functions and showed you how to get help with a known command, how to find the commands that relate to a certain "theme" if you don't know what command does what, and how to use tools like `Show-Command` to help you structure commands correctly. You learned a lot here! Pat yourself on the back, but don't stop your learning now—let's keep going.

Chapter 3
The PowerShell Pipeline

Welcome to Chapter 3 of *Learning PowerShell*. In this chapter, I am going to show you one of the most important features of PowerShell, which is the ability to chain commands together to accomplish some really big task. This is one of the most valuable things you can learn about PowerShell and, with this tool in hand, you can manage to accomplish a lot of menial tasks with just a little work. Without further ado, let's get started.

Introducing the Pipeline

The *pipeline* in PowerShell is essentially how you glue stuff together in your scripting—or, more specifically, how you take the output or results from one PowerShell command and send it into another for further processing. The process of using the pipeline is called piping, and of course the invisible tube that connects one command to another is the pipeline. The character that represents all this:

```
|
```

It's the one under the Backspace key on most keyboards.

In this case, I think the best way to show off the pipeline is to start with a simple example. But before we do that, I need to introduce two helpful commands in PowerShell:

- `Format-List`, which takes the output of almost any cmdlet and formats it in a list that explodes all relevant details; and
- `Format-Table`, which formats output in a nice text-based table.

`Format-List` and `Format-Table` are absolutely dependent on the pipeline. You can't just issue a `Format-List` command, because there has to be data to format in the first place. You get that data to the `Format-List` command through the pipeline.

Recall from Chapters 1 and 2 that I often referred to the `Get-Process` command, which lists the running processes on a system. If we ran `Get-Help Get-Process`, we would see the following:

```
NAME
     Get-Process
```

DOI 10.1515/9781501506673-003

SYNOPSIS
    Gets the processes that are running on the local
computer or a remote computer.

SYNTAX
    Get-Process [[-Name] [<String[]>]] [-ComputerName
[<String[]>]] [-FileVersionInfo] [-InformationAction
    {SilentlyContinue | Stop | Continue | Inquire |
Ignore | Suspend}] [-InformationVariable [<Sys-
tem.String]>]]
    [-Module] [<CommonParameters>]

You can see that there's a parameter called -Name which is actually for the name of a process running on a system. I can tell that, because if I look one parameter over, I see there is -ComputerName, so I can puzzle out that that parameter is for looking at running processes on a given computer. The -Name parameter, I can then surmise, must be for examining something about a process that I can select by name.

Does it work? Well, let's kill two birds with one stone: let's practice pipelining by asking Get-Process to give us more information on the Chrome process, but let's get that extra information formatted nice and neatly as a list:

Get-Process chrome | Format-List

Here is what PowerShell returns to me:

```
Id        : 132
Handles   : 224
CPU       : 0.1875
Name      : chrome

Id        : 8428
Handles   : 997
CPU       : 1.4375
Name      : chrome

Id        : 10440
```

```
Handles : 247
CPU     : 1.546875
Name    : chrome
```

There are all the Chrome processes on my machine right now, formatted as a list, with some of their properties exposed and expanded. To recap, we got here by taking the output of Get-Process chrome and piping it using the | character into the Format-List cmdlet.

Let's think about another example, also using a command I have used in Chapters 1 and 2: the Get-EventLog command. Remember we can get the last 10 events in the security event log on the current computer by simply popping the following command into the console:

```
Get-EventLog -Log Name security -Newest 5
```

Right now, that command gives me the following output:

```
  Index Time           Entry Type   Source            Instanced
Message
  ----- ----           ---------    ------            ----------
-------
   8632 Nov 09 15:50  Success... Microsoft-Windows...      4798
A user's local group membership was enumerated....
   8631 Nov 09 15:28 Failure... Microsoft-Windows...       5061
Cryptographic operation....
   8630 Nov 09 15:28 Success... Microsoft-Windows...       5058
Key file operation....
   8629 Nov 09 14:09 Success... Microsoft-Windows...       4672
Special privileges assigned to new logon....
   8628 Nov 09 14:09 Success... Microsoft-Windows...       4624
An account was successfully logged on....
```

Great. But I want to know about that failure message, which I can see is number 8631. So I want to get information about that event and get its details. How do you think I would do that? Here's the thought process that I would use. First, I would see if Get-EventLog permitted me to just specify an event ID, which it looks like is called the Index from the table I see above. So in the console, I'll type in Show-Command Get-EventLog and I get the dialog box in Figure 3.1.

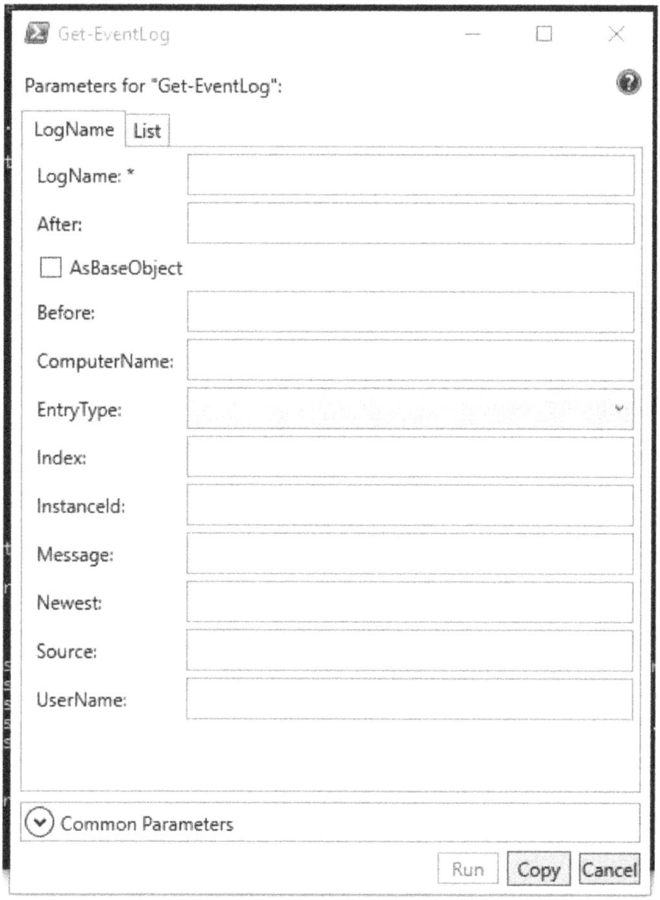

Figure 3.1: How can I use Get-EventLog just to check out one event from the Security event log?

Sure enough, while I see the -LogName parameter is required, because it has an asterisk next to it, I can also see that Index is a supported parameter because it shows up there on the screen. So I'll type in "Security" in the LogName parameter field, and I'll use the index number I already saw above, which was 8631. Then I'll click the Run button in the lower right-hand corner of the dialog box, and I'll look to see what PowerShell has for me in the console window, which you can see in Figure 3.2.

```
PS C:\users\jon\desktop> show-command get-eventlog
PS C:\users\jon\desktop> Get-EventLog -LogName Security -Index 8631

   Index Time            EntryType  Source                    InstanceID Message
   ----- ----            ---------  ------                    ---------- -------
    8631 Nov 09 15:28   FailureA... Microsoft-Windows...            5061 Cryptographic operation....
```

Figure 3.2: The result returned from Show-Command Get-EventLog, after I filled everything out.

Note: Sometimes, especially in Windows 10, the Show-Command dialog box will return the properly formatted command to the console window except for a stray ^M at the end. You will need to delete that ^M before you can hit Enter to run the command, or you may get an error. Hopefully, this bug is fixed in one of the future releases of Windows 10.

Boom! That's a properly formatted command. But now how might I get more details on that? Well, I'd format that as a list, not as a table, so I can see more properties and extended information about that specific event. To do that, I'd use the pipeline and pipe the output of my command to the Format-List command, as you see in Figure 3.3.

```
PS C:\users\jon\desktop> Get-EventLog -LogName Security -Index 8631 | Format-List

Index              : 8631
EntryType          : FailureAudit
InstanceId         : 5061
Message            : Cryptographic operation.

                     Subject:
                        Security ID:          S-1-5-18
                        Account Name:         JON-LAPTOP$
                        Account Domain:       HASSELL
                        Logon ID:             0x3e7

                     Cryptographic Parameters:
                        Provider Name:    Microsoft Software Key Storage Provider
                        Algorithm Name:       RSA
                        Key Name:         51a92691-66f1-280f-d0db-59fad4f73491
                        Key Type:         %%2500

                     Cryptographic Operation:
                        Operation:        %%2480
                        Return Code:          0x80090016
Category           : (12290)
CategoryNumber     : 12290
ReplacementStrings : {S-1-5-18, JON-LAPTOP$, HASSELL, 0x3e7...}
Source             : Microsoft-Windows-Security-Auditing
TimeGenerated      : 11/9/2015 3:28:18 PM
TimeWritten        : 11/9/2015 3:28:18 PM
UserName           :
```

Figure 3.3: Success, since I have information on a single event formatted nicely into a list.

I've successfully used the pipeline in that example, too.

One thing to note in general about the pipeline: commands that share nouns will generally support the fullest passing of information between them using the pipeline. `Get-Process` and `Set-Process`, for example, would support a lot of information being passed between them. `Get-Mailbox`, `Set-Mailbox`, `Export-Mailbox`, `Import-Mailbox` are all examples of the most compatible pipeline sharing commands because they all share the "mailbox" noun. Sometimes if you string together completely unrelated commands in a pipeline, it won't work, or PowerShell will do something drastic and completely unintended. We call these types of commands "weekend killers," because you know who is going to be cleaning up the side effects of a bad command late on Saturday night. Other commands, as I have shown here, also support passing information, but the noun sharing ones will have the most useful sharing support.

Piping to the Screen and to Files

You are using the pipeline all the time when you run single commands in PowerShell. Fun fact!

To the Screen: `Out-Host`

All commands have, by default, an invisible but still very real command attached to them, called `Out-Host`. So whenever you run single commands, PowerShell is putting a "| `Out-Host`" to the end of it. `Out-Host` sends output directly to the console screen.

You normally won't have a lot of use for `Out-Host` in single command scenarios, although you will find the command useful when you start putting together advanced scripts. Most scripters use the command to write messages to the user while the script is running, to say things like "executing this stage of the operation; please wait" or similar. It's a good way to keep the user engaged and remove any suspicion that a script has hung or stalled, and it's an easy way to communicate with the person running the script. But again, that's for scripts, not really for a lot of single-use commands like you will be experiencing as a beginner.

If there is `Out-Host`, then what other Out-style commands might there be? Do you remember how we discussed finding new commands when you have the general concept of what you want to get done? A quick memory jog: we can search the `Get-Command` command using wildcards. Let's try:

```
Get-Command *out*
```

Specifically, though, Get-Command has a parameter called -Verb, which lets you search through commands that have the verb portions of their names matching whatever keyword you select. So here, we would use
```
Get-Command -verb *Out*
```

What does that result look like? You can see in Figure 3.4.

```
PS C:\Users\Jon> Get-Command -verb *Out*

CommandType     Name                          Version     Source
-----------     ----                          -------     ------
Cmdlet          Out-Default                   3.0.0.0     Microsoft.PowerShell.Core
Cmdlet          Out-File                      3.1.0.0     Microsoft.PowerShell.Utility
Cmdlet          Out-GridView                  3.1.0.0     Microsoft.PowerShell.Utility
Cmdlet          Out-Host                      3.0.0.0     Microsoft.PowerShell.Core
Cmdlet          Out-Null                      3.0.0.0     Microsoft.PowerShell.Core
Cmdlet          Out-Printer                   3.1.0.0     Microsoft.PowerShell.Utility
Cmdlet          Out-String                    3.1.0.0     Microsoft.PowerShell.Utility
```

Figure 3.4: Finding other destinations to which I can pipe output.

Looks like we have seven options. To beginners, two of those are going to be particularly interesting.

To Files: Out-File

Out-File is sort of the like the > character used in DOS commands: it directs the output of your command to a file. In fact, you can simply use the DOS > character inside PowerShell a lot of the time, but piping the output of one command to Out-File and then naming that file are the proper way to do it.

You would use something like, say, Get-Mailbox | Out-File mailboxes.txt to get a list of Exchange mailboxes and export them to a text file.

Out-File essentially sends a text-based copy of whatever the console output would be to a specified file, as simple as that. The output will be 80 columns wide and, if necessary (depending on your geographic location and the language which your system uses), Out-File lets you specify different character encodings. You can also use the command to add content to the end of an existing file; Out-File knows not to overwrite any content already in a file and will politely add to the end of a running file, which can be very helpful in situations where you might need a transcript of your commands or any other sort of breadcrumb situation.

To Printers: `Out-Printer`

As you might expect, `Out-Printer` will send output to printers. Specifically, the command will send output to the default printer set up on the system or to an alternate printer, if one is specified. You specify the name of the printer by what it is named in Control Panel > Printers, depending on your version of Windows. What a great time to use the "tab to complete" feature of the Windows PowerShell console if you don't remember the name of the printer!

Here's how you would use this to send that same list of Exchange mailboxes to the default printer on your system:

```
Get-Mailbox | Out-Printer
```

Importing and Exporting Data for PowerShell to Work With

The pipeline is also a primary way that you can put data into PowerShell and get it out again, as needed. For instance, you might need to read in a list of something, do some commands, filter some stuff, do some more commands on the refined list, and then spit out some confirmation that whatever you wanted changed was changed by the system. Or maybe you need to export some data from, say, Active Directory, import it into an Office 365 PowerShell session and read that data into the cloud and report back. There are several reasons why you might need to import and export data, and PowerShell comes built-in with a number of ways to handle both scenarios.

First off, let's get a sense of the universe of commands that import and export things. You should know by now how we might find this information out. How do we find a list of all commands that import something? How do we find a list of all commands that export something?

That's right, `Get-Command` and some wildcards will get us where we need to be.

Figure 3.5 shows what both `Get-Command -verb *Import*` and `Get-Command -verb *Export*` return on my Windows 10 system here:

```
PS C:\Users\Jon> Get-Command -verb *Import*

CommandType     Name                        Version   Source
-----------     ----                        -------   ------
Function        Import-BCCachePackage       1.0.0.0   BranchCache
Function        Import-BCSecretKey          1.0.0.0   BranchCache
Function        Import-IseSnippet           1.0.0.0   ISE
Cmdlet          Import-Alias                3.1.0.0   Microsoft.PowerShell.Utility
Cmdlet          Import-BinaryMiLog          1.0.0.0   CimCmdlets
Cmdlet          Import-Certificate          1.0.0.0   PKI
Cmdlet          Import-Clixml               3.1.0.0   Microsoft.PowerShell.Utility
Cmdlet          Import-Counter              3.0.0.0   Microsoft.PowerShell.Diagnostics
Cmdlet          Import-Csv                  3.1.0.0   Microsoft.PowerShell.Utility
Cmdlet          Import-LocalizedData        3.1.0.0   Microsoft.PowerShell.Utility
Cmdlet          Import-Module               3.0.0.0   Microsoft.PowerShell.Core
Cmdlet          Import-PfxCertificate       1.0.0.0   PKI
Cmdlet          Import-PSSession            3.1.0.0   Microsoft.PowerShell.Utility
Cmdlet          Import-StartLayout          1.0.0.0   StartLayout
Cmdlet          Import-TpmOwnerAuth         2.0.0.0   TrustedPlatformModule


PS C:\Users\Jon> Get-Command -verb *Export*

CommandType     Name                        Version   Source
-----------     ----                        -------   ------
Function        Export-BCCachePackage       1.0.0.0   BranchCache
Function        Export-BCSecretKey          1.0.0.0   BranchCache
Function        Export-ODataEndpointProxy   1.0       Microsoft.PowerShell.ODataUtils
Function        Export-ScheduledTask        1.0.0.0   ScheduledTasks
Cmdlet          Export-Alias                3.1.0.0   Microsoft.PowerShell.Utility
Cmdlet          Export-BinaryMiLog          1.0.0.0   CimCmdlets
Cmdlet          Export-Certificate          1.0.0.0   PKI
Cmdlet          Export-Clixml               3.1.0.0   Microsoft.PowerShell.Utility
Cmdlet          Export-Console              3.0.0.0   Microsoft.PowerShell.Core
Cmdlet          Export-Counter              3.0.0.0   Microsoft.PowerShell.Diagnostics
Cmdlet          Export-Csv                  3.1.0.0   Microsoft.PowerShell.Utility
Cmdlet          Export-FormatData           3.1.0.0   Microsoft.PowerShell.Utility
Cmdlet          Export-ModuleMember         3.0.0.0   Microsoft.PowerShell.Core
Cmdlet          Export-PfxCertificate       1.0.0.0   PKI
Cmdlet          Export-PSSession            3.1.0.0   Microsoft.PowerShell.Utility
Cmdlet          Export-StartLayout          1.0.0.0   StartLayout
Cmdlet          Export-TlsSessionTicketKey  2.0.0.0   TLS
Cmdlet          Export-WindowsDriver        3.0       Dism
Cmdlet          Export-WindowsImage         3.0       Dism
```

Figure 3.5: Finding a list of commands that import and export things.

A rule of thumb, which is not always true but is true enough to be useful: import commands and export commands are generally twins, so both will exist for any given noun, with some exceptions. This is particularly true of third party modules, like those that import commands for Office 365, Exchange, SharePoint, Skype for Business, and so on. But rare is the instance where you can bring something into PowerShell but you can't get it out, or where you can't bring something into PowerShell but can export it once it's in a different format. It generally does not happen.

The import and export commands all pay attention to the type of file being imported and exported, and then they use PowerShell's built-in interpreters and parsers to read the type of file and glean its contents and other information based on the file's use of a known and consistent format. All of this is to say that you need to use the right import and export command for the file type in question, and if you use an export command, then use the corresponding import command. Conversely, if you use an import command, you would want to use the corresponding export command in most cases. And, don't really think of using the Get-Content command for anything but text files. That command knows how to read only plain text, and it won't do any parsing or interpreting of any other formats for you.

Importing from Comma-Separated Values (CSV) Files

One of the biggest uses of the import and export features are in dealing with comma-separated values files, which are great ways to describe a bunch of like-organized material, such as lists of users, mailboxes, files, groups, and so on.

A quick primer about CSVs: they are structured as basically text files. The first row of the text file is the header and it describes the data in columns, separating each "column" with a comma. Each subsequent row is the actual data, again with the records being separated into columns with commas. Here is a sample CSV file:

```
Name,PhoneNumber,Email,alias
Jon Hassell,7041234567,jon@jonathanhassell.com,jhas-
sell
Tom Cruise,2121234567,tom@cruise.com,tcruise
George Clooney,,georgeclooney@hollywood.com,gclooney
```

You can see for George Clooney's record that I don't have a phone number. That's OK because I've just added another comma, which means "no data here, just keep going."

Go ahead and use that example above to create your own CSV file. You can retype it or cut and paste it into Notepad, and then just save that file as "list.csv"—be sure to use the quotes so that Notepad knows to save the file with that extension.

Let's try out the Import-CSV command. Open the console and navigate to the directory to which you saved your CSV file. Then just type in:

```
Import-CSV list.csv
```

You'll get back something that should make you happy, as you see from Figure 3.6:

```
PS C:\Users\Jon> Import-CSV .\list.csv

Name            PhoneNumber Email                         alias
----            ----------- -----                         -----
Jon Hassell     7041234567  jon@jonathanhassell.com       jhassell
Tom Cruise      2121234567  tom@cruise.com                tcruise
George Clooney              georgeclooney@hollywood.com   gclooney
```

Figure 3.6: Importing a CSV file via a PowerShell console command.

It's a properly formatted table. PowerShell did the hard work of parsing the CSV file, reading in the data, and formatting it to the screen. It did that because it knows how to read, parse, and interpret CSV files.

Can we use the pipeline to do something with this? Absolutely. Recall from earlier in this chapter the `Format-List` command, which formats rows of data into a nice, neat list for easy viewing. Since PowerShell has by default imported our CSV file as a table, we can use the pipeline to pipe the output of the `Import-CSV` command to `Format-List` so that we can view the contents of our imported CSV file in a different style.

```
Import-CSV list.csv | Format-List
```

Figure 3.7 demonstrates what PowerShell returns.

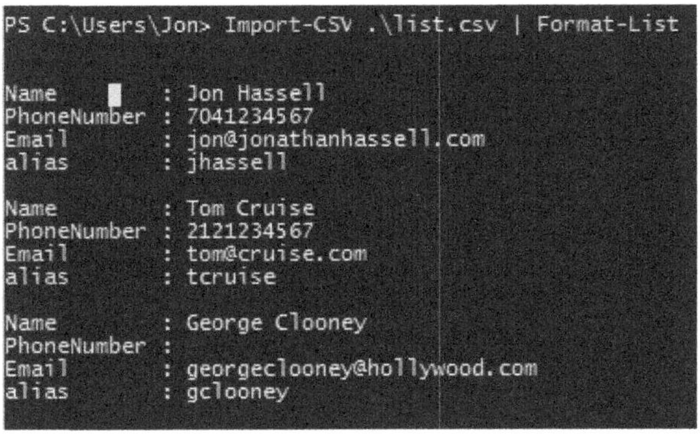

```
PS C:\Users\Jon> Import-CSV .\list.csv | Format-List

Name        : Jon Hassell
PhoneNumber : 7041234567
Email       : jon@jonathanhassell.com
alias       : jhassell

Name        : Tom Cruise
PhoneNumber : 2121234567
Email       : tom@cruise.com
alias       : tcruise

Name        : George Clooney
PhoneNumber :
Email       : georgeclooney@hollywood.com
alias       : gclooney
```

Figure 3.7: Piping an imported CSV file to a different command to format it in a new way.

Notice again how the missing entry for George Clooney's phone number is handled gracefully.

Exporting to Comma-Separated Values (CSV) Files

What happens if we want to export to a CSV? Let's start with a different example. Maybe we want to create a short cheat sheet we can print out and paste on our desks when we're working with PowerShell's various import commands. We'll use `Get-Command` to get a list of import commands and then pipe it to `Export-CSV`, where we'll supply a name for a CSV file, and then we can look at the contents and use Excel to format it and add some notes of our own.

```
Get-Command -verb *Import* | Export-CSV importcom-
mands.csv
```

To examine the CSV that's generated, you can just type in `notepad import-commands.csv` to load Notepad with the CSV file already opened. Figure 3.8 shows what that looks like:

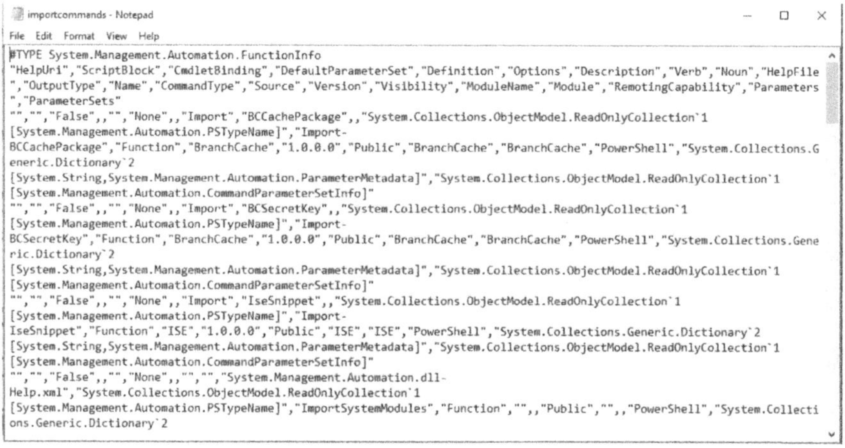

Figure 3.8: The CSV file we just generated.

We can then open that file in Excel and add columns for our own notes, cheats, and more. We can also remove the columns we don't care about and further format the list for printing, as shown in Figure 3.9.

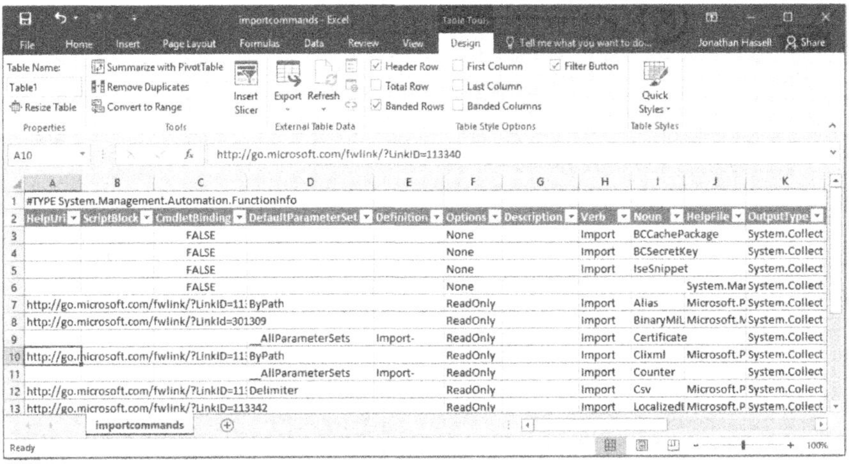

Figure 3.9: The CSV file we just generated, opened in Excel and further formatted.

As you can see, it's easy to work with CSV files in PowerShell. Most of the time, you'll import and export these CSV files, and indeed many other types of files, while using the pipeline to perform some functions or other work on the data or content that was imported.

Converting Content

Sometimes you might find it useful to transform content from one form to another. In the examples above, we were using CSV files exclusively and while the data was formatted on the screen in a nice table, ultimately PowerShell was still interpreting and parsing the CSV format and not translating it into something else. For instance, what if we wanted to take that CSV file and turn it into a web page? What if we have an XML file from one business system or another, and we need to do something with it in PowerShell and then return a CSV? For that, we need to *convert* content, and luckily PowerShell has the built-in ability to handle that scenario.

You can convert content with the `ConvertTo-` series of commands. Quick quiz: how would you find out what these are? Don't look ahead: we've used this technique a couple of times in this chapter, so you should be able to puzzle it out. I'll wait here.

Insert Jeopardy theme music.

OK, we're back. You would use

```
Get-Command -verb *ConvertTo*
```

And Figure 3.10 shows what that command returns to your console screen:

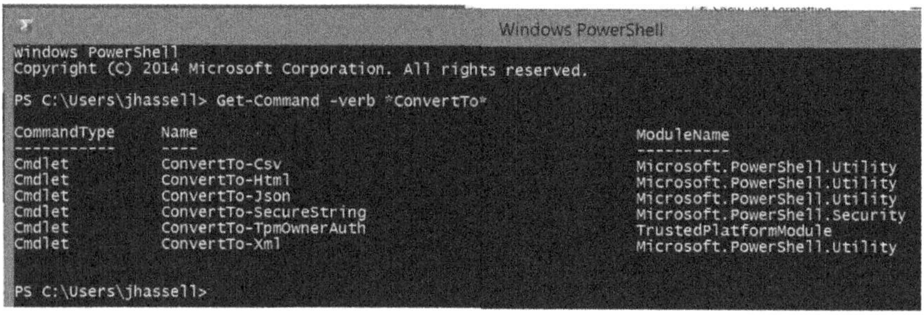

Figure 3.10: Getting a list of ConvertTo commands that are available for use.

There are three results here that are interesting to us as beginning PowerShell students. First, there's ConvertTo-Csv, which as you might expect will turn a table of information into a CSV file. This is useful when you want to dump a bunch of like data into a file that you can import into Excel or SQL Server and run a bunch of analyses and number crunching on it. There is also ConvertTo-Html, which formats output as a modestly styled but reasonable web page with a single command. Finally, there is ConvertTo-Xml, which is a useful way of communicating information between disparate systems. When you start writing advanced configuration scripts and shipping log information and configuration documents between systems for installation and deployment purposes, you probably will use the XML conversion feature a lot.

It is important to note that these conversion commands work only with the data and the content already within PowerShell's memory, the data that is in your current session. You will not want to display most of these conversions on the screen only; instead, you'll want to write them to disk. The Convert commands do not write anything to disk—they merely convert the format. The Export commands we worked with earlier *do* in fact write to disk, so this is a key distinction to make. When working with the conversion commands, you'll need to use a now familiar command, Out-File, as we talked about earlier in this chapter, to get the conversion out to disk where you can move it, copy it, open it in another application, or do whatever you need to with it.

Let's try this on for size. Remember in Chapter 2, where we were using the Get-EventLog command? Let's try to export the newest five entries from the

Application event log to an HTML file using a conversion command, but we also need to keep in mind that since the conversion command only keeps the results in memory, we need to get those results into a file. We'll use `Out-File` for that.

```
Get-EventLog -LogName Application -Newest 5 | ConvertTo-
Html | Out-File newest5app.html
```

I'll open this file in Firefox, my web browser of choice, to see the final result of that command. You can take a gander at the result in Figure 3.11.

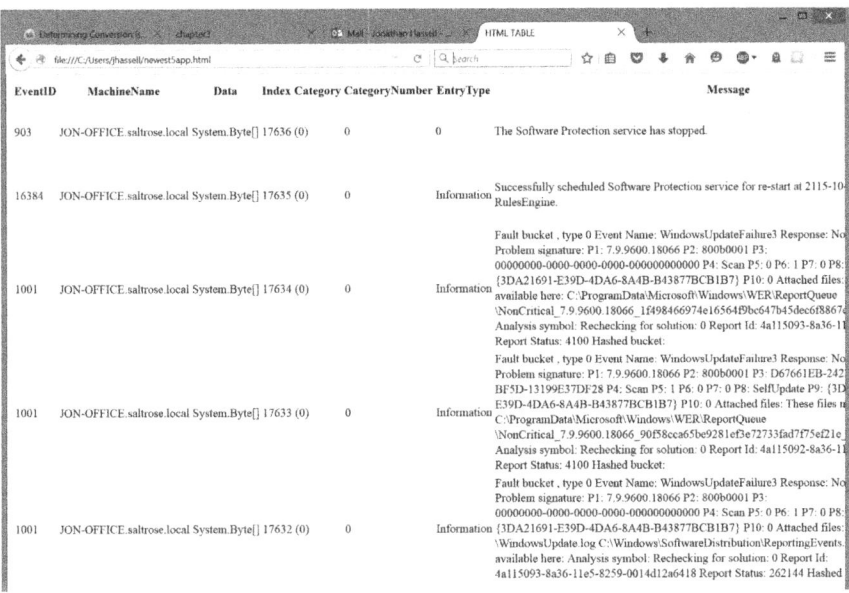

Figure 3.11: The HTML-converted output from a PowerShell command.

The Last Word

As I mentioned, my goal for this chapter of *Learning PowerShell* was to show you one of the most important features of PowerShell, the ability to chain commands together to accomplish some big task. This is one of the most valuable things you can learn about PowerShell and with this tool in hand, you can manage to accomplish a lot of menial tasks with just a little work. We looked at how to use the pipeline and how the pipeline works in conjunction with writing output to the screen, to files, to printers, and how to get data to and from files of different formats and types. This is a key, fundamental part of PowerShell, and now you know all about it. Congratulations!

Chapter 4
PowerShell Providers, Modules, and Snap-ins

Welcome to Chapter 4 of *Learning PowerShell*! In this chapter, I am going to show you another of the most important features of PowerShell: providers, modules, and snap-ins. These are really the core of the universe when it comes to all the commands available for use within PowerShell, so I want to teach you what they are, how they work, and how to use them in your daily activities. Let's dive in!

Introducing Providers

When you hear the term "providers," I bet the non-developers among us (and I include myself in this group) start to tune out. That sounds like something you do along with creating a class and instantiating a `for` loop with strings that pass through a model view controller. But let me simplify this for you a bit, at least in the context of PowerShell.

PowerShell providers are essentially like drivers for the operating system, where you install some code to help your copy of Windows talk to the graphics hardware, the storage and disk subsystem, and the chipset on your motherboard. The drivers contain the "translation layer," which is not an official term, so that Windows knows how to drive the hardware and make it work for your use. PowerShell providers are drivers for PowerShell to navigate things besides the file system. Providers allow PowerShell to traverse the Registry, the File System, Windows Management Instrumentation (WMI) functionality, and more. Third parties can create providers: for example, there is a SQL Server provider that Microsoft installs that lets you do PowerShell operations on databases.

How Providers Work

How does it work? Providers take some collection of something, whatever resource they are trying to enable for PowerShell management, and make it look like a file system or disk drive to PowerShell. Providers are used by all sorts of software packages that support PowerShell for administration, like Internet Information Services (Microsoft's web server) and Active Directory. This is one of PowerShell's key extensibility features, because any resource or data to be managed always shows up like a drive. In addition, new commands can be added that

DOI 10.1515/9781501506673-004

interact with the same data storage, whether that's a database or a list of administrative settings for a website or a mailbox store or anything else, really. It's kind of cool.

How do you know what providers you already have? PowerShell does indeed ship with some. What command might you use to find out how to deal with providers? That's right:

```
Get-Command -noun *Provider*
```

That returns what you see in Figure 4.1.

```
PS C:\Users\jhassell> Get-Command -noun *Provider*

CommandType     Name                                        ModuleName
-----------     ----                                        ----------
Function        Add-NetEventPacketCaptureProvider           NetEventPacketCapture
Function        Add-NetEventProvider                        NetEventPacketCapture
Function        Get-NetEventPacketCaptureProvider           NetEventPacketCapture
Function        Get-NetEventProvider                        NetEventPacketCapture
Function        Get-StorageProvider                         Storage
Function        Remove-NetEventPacketCaptureProvider        NetEventPacketCapture
Function        Remove-NetEventProvider                     NetEventPacketCapture
Function        Set-NetEventPacketCaptureProvider           NetEventPacketCapture
Function        Set-NetEventProvider                        NetEventPacketCapture
Function        Set-StorageProvider                         Storage
Function        Update-StorageProviderCache                 Storage
Cmdlet          Get-PSProvider                              Microsoft.PowerShell.Management
```

Figure 4.1: The help returned from `Get-Command -noun *Provider*`.

Which one looks like the command we want? The last one, `Get-PSProvider`, seems to really be what we want. I'll just run that from the console without any parameters to get a look at what providers I already have. Figure 4.2 shows the result.

```
PS C:\Windows\system32> Get-PSProvider

Name            Capabilities                               Drives
----            ------------                               ------
Alias           ShouldProcess                              {Alias}
Environment     ShouldProcess                              {Env}
FileSystem      Filter, ShouldProcess, Credentials         {C, D, E}
Function        ShouldProcess                              {Function}
Registry        ShouldProcess, Transactions                {HKLM, HKCU}
Variable        ShouldProcess                              {Variable}
```

Figure 4.2: Looking at providers already installed on the system.

Provider Capabilities and Drives

The names of the providers are fairly obvious. It looks like PowerShell can make aliases, the environment (which is environmental variables like PATH and more), the FileSystem, functions, the Registry, and any defined variables all look like disk drives, so I can reach in and touch data or records in any one of these "places" just by "cd:"-ing around and adding path-like statements to get to where I want to be. When you use a provider, you are technically creating a PSDrive, and that PSDrive is the representation of the storage or resource you are connecting to as the file system on a disk.

The other columns in the list are *capabilities* and *drives*. *Capabilities* are a list of ways to use and things you can (and can't) do with each provider. They include:

- **ShouldProcess.** This means that the provider supports the `-whatif` and `-confirm` parameters, the big risk-mitigation parameters common to cmdlets using the providers.
- **Filter.** This indicates that you can filter the items that come out of working with that provider (more on filtering later). More importantly, it means you can reduce a large working set to something smaller or more defined based on some common characteristic.
- **Credentials.** You can use the `-credential` parameter when working with this provider's cmdlets to use a different security identity to connect to its storage collection. This is useful in file system contexts for setting and testing permissions or gaining access to remote disk storage.
- **Transactions.** This indicates support for ensuring several things complete before committing a transaction and rolling all operations back to original state before stopping. Transaction support is particularly good for data-integrity operations.

Drives, on the other hand, are the logical access point for providers. They're like drive mappings in Windows that you would use to make, say, Drive M: represent a share (and its contents) on another computer. For instance, if we were working with the Registry provider, the drive letter used to spelunk around and do things would be HKLM and HKCU. So we might want to change "directory" to HKLM and do a directory listing to see what was available to manage, in which case we would use the `Set-Location` cmdlet to change the shell's current container to the container you want. Here's what that looks like when I issue `Set-Location hklm:` at the prompt; take a look at Figure 4.3.

Linux Equivalent of CD command.
Hive Key Local machine

```
PS C:\Windows\system32> set-location hklm:
PS HKLM:\> dir


    Hive: HKEY_LOCAL_MACHINE


Name                                    Property
----                                    --------
BCD00000000
HARDWARE
SAM
dir : Requested registry access is not allowed.
At line:1 char:1
+ dir
+ ~~~
    + CategoryInfo          : PermissionDenied: (HKEY_LOCAL_MACHINE\SECURITY:String) [Get-ChildItem], SecurityExceptio
   n
    + FullyQualifiedErrorId : System.Security.SecurityException,Microsoft.PowerShell.Commands.GetChildItemCommand

SOFTWARE                                (default) :
SYSTEM

PS HKLM:\>
```

Figure 4.3: Changing "directories" to the Registry via the PowerShell Registry provider.

You can see that `dir` listed out the main areas of the Registry, including HKEY_LOCAL_MACHINE, HKEY_CURRENT_USER, and so on. You work the tree by using it like a file system. Is this starting to make sense to you?

Items

As far as interacting with providers goes, you generally use the *item* set of cmdlets to interact with PSDrive providers. If you continue to consider working with providers like working with a file system, then instead of files and folders, think items. Calling Registry keys or SQL Server databases "files" and "folders" is a little weird. Items is a nice generic term that can be used interchangeably.

How do you figure out what the item cmdlets are? Why, you'd use `Get-Command`, of course! Look at the example in Figure 4.4.

The ones we care about are the cmdlets. Looks like we can clear the value of items, copy them, get information about them, start them, move them, create new items, remove and rename items, set them, and more.

Most of the `item` set of cmdlets have a -`path` parameter that accepts wildcards like *, but this brings up an important point. Precisely because providers support so many different types of storage and resources, there may be cases in which the wildcard is actually a valid, legal, specific input for a given provider—in which case, if you use it with PowerShell, it will get confused. For providers that allow the standard wildcard characters as legal characters in names, you can use the -`literalpath` instead of just -`path` to tell PowerShell to treat the asterisk as an asterisk and not as a wildcard.

```
PS C:\Windows\system32> Get-Command -noun *Item*

CommandType     Name                              ModuleName
-----------     ----                              ----------
Function        Get-DAEntryPointTableItem         DirectAccessClientComponents
Function        New-DAEntryPointTableItem         DirectAccessClientComponents
Function        Remove-DAEntryPointTableItem      DirectAccessClientComponents
Function        Rename-DAEntryPointTableItem      DirectAccessClientComponents
Function        Reset-DAEntryPointTableItem       DirectAccessClientComponents
Function        Set-DAEntryPointTableItem         DirectAccessClientComponents
Cmdlet          Clear-Item                        Microsoft.PowerShell.Management
Cmdlet          Clear-ItemProperty                Microsoft.PowerShell.Management
Cmdlet          Copy-Item                         Microsoft.PowerShell.Management
Cmdlet          Copy-ItemProperty                 Microsoft.PowerShell.Management
Cmdlet          Get-ChildItem                     Microsoft.PowerShell.Management
Cmdlet          Get-ControlPanelItem              Microsoft.PowerShell.Management
Cmdlet          Get-Item                          Microsoft.PowerShell.Management
Cmdlet          Get-ItemProperty                  Microsoft.PowerShell.Management
Cmdlet          Invoke-Item                       Microsoft.PowerShell.Management
Cmdlet          Move-Item                         Microsoft.PowerShell.Management
Cmdlet          Move-ItemProperty                 Microsoft.PowerShell.Management
Cmdlet          New-Item                          Microsoft.PowerShell.Management
Cmdlet          New-ItemProperty                  Microsoft.PowerShell.Management
Cmdlet          Remove-Item                       Microsoft.PowerShell.Management
Cmdlet          Remove-ItemProperty               Microsoft.PowerShell.Management
Cmdlet          Rename-Item                       Microsoft.PowerShell.Management
Cmdlet          Rename-ItemProperty               Microsoft.PowerShell.Management
Cmdlet          Set-Item                          Microsoft.PowerShell.Management
Cmdlet          Set-ItemProperty                  Microsoft.PowerShell.Management
Cmdlet          Show-ControlPanelItem             Microsoft.PowerShell.Management
```

Figure 4.4: Examining the item set of cmdlets for working with PowerShell providers.

Let's dig in a little further to items. Items have properties, which are basically characteristics about the item. If I have a file, then I have the date that file was created (a property), the date it was modified (a property), whether or not it is read-only or writeable (a property), and so on. If I have a Registry key, I have its location (a property), its type (a property), and so on. Items can also have child items, or items within that item. Again using the file system example, folders can have folders within them and within a folder can be files.

When you want to create a new item, in many cases you have to tell PowerShell what kind of item to create. For example, the `Show-Command` entry for `New-Item` demonstrates that `-ItemType` is a parameter I can specify. PowerShell sometimes tries to guess what kind of item you should create based on the provider you are currently working with, but it doesn't always guess correctly. So if I'm in C:\Windows\System32 and I want to create a new directory called jhtest with PowerShell, I would use `New-Item -Path jhtest -ItemType directory` so PowerShell knows that I would want a directory and not a file. If you don't specify, then PowerShell will give you a little prompt that looks like

`Type:`

And you will need to specify the type of new item that you want to create.

Differences in Providers Matter

It is important to remember that in PowerShell, not every provider has the same capabilities. Some work when others don't, depending on the scenario. Some providers let you access different things than others; some do it in different ways; and some don't work at all. That's why you always have to think about what capabilities each provider has when building commands using a PSDrive provider, and you must always remember that when you are working with a provider with which you are unfamiliar, be sure to run `Get-PSProvider` to understand its capabilities. Even if a command seems like it would work, the context of the provider in which you are running that command matters a great deal.

A Provider Example: The Registry

The best way to learn is with a hands-on example, and I can think of one no better than changing the Registry exclusively through the use of PowerShell. Our task? Turn off Wi-Fi Sense in Windows 10.

Note: What is Windows 10 Wi-Fi Sense? It is Windows 10 automatically sharing wireless network passwords with your friends. It's wrong and a big security problem and you should just turn it off.

Surely, since Wi-Fi Sense is a configuration setting within the Windows operating system, the actual place that setting and its status are stored is in the Registry. I Googled around for a couple of minutes and found that, at least in the RTM build of Windows 10 (build 10240 to be exact), the Registry setting for this feature was at

```
HKEY_LOCAL_MACHINE\SOFTWARE\Microsoft\WcmSvc\wifinet-
workmanager\config\
```

The actual setting is controlled by a DWORD value called, affectionately, `Auto-ConnectAllowedOEM` and, to turn it off, we need to set its value to 0.

Now that the task has been laid out before us, it's time to get to work. From a PowerShell console, let's get into the PSDrive for the Registry.

```
Set-Location -path HKLM:
```

You can do a quick `dir` to make sure you're in the right spot. You can also notice that the PowerShell prompt changes to `HKLM` to reflect your current location. It's all good right now. Let's go ahead and get further into the Registry, all the way down to the location I identified above that I got from my Google research:

```
Set-location path hklm:\ SOFTWARE\Mi-
crosoft\WcmSvc\wifinetworkmanager\config\
```

Let's do another quick `dir` to see what there is to see. From the report, do you see the value `AutoConnectAllowedOEM` that we need to create?

I don't, so that means we actually need to create the value. For this, we would use ...yes, the `New-Item` cmdlet. Here are a few ways we could go about this:

— `New-Item` alone at the command prompt with nothing else would prompt PowerShell to prompt us (that's a lot of prompting, folks!) for all of the required parameters.

— We could use `Get-Help New-Item` to read about what we could do with this command.

— We could also use `Show-Command new-item` to guide us graphically.

Use whichever of those combinations feels right to you. In any case, you should end up alongside me with the following command put together:

```
New-Item -path AutoConnectAllowedOEM -type DWORD -
value 0
```

In the case of this specific `New-Item` command, `-Path` is the name of the key that we want to create, since the path refers to the way to get to the object. We're creating a new DWORD object in the Registry, so `-type` would be DWORD, and of course we know from our research that the `-value` of this new key would need to be 0.

Voila! You have successfully managed the Registry using nothing but PowerShell. But just think for a minute: literally every configuration setting within the Windows operating system is managed through the Registry, so that means you just gained the skill to interact with and change Registry settings exclusively through scripting. More power to you!

Introducing Modules and Snap-ins

I know that I keep saying I am going to introduce you to one of PowerShell's most important features, but in truth they are all important. The modules feature, however, is where PowerShell gets its ability to address a ton of different products and services from within one shell environment. Adding modules lets PowerShell work with different features, functions, and configurations from all sorts of different software, both from Microsoft and from third parties, just by importing modules full of cmdlets and their reference information or by adding a snap-in.

What are modules? What are snap-ins? Let's do some rudimentary definition work upfront so we can get it out of the way.

— **Modules.** Modules are nice, neat containers of PowerShell functionality that extend the namespace and targeting power of PowerShell to other pieces of hardware and software. Modules are the de facto way of enabling PowerShell extensibility these days, and most server products that run on Windows come with modules for extending PowerShell, including all Microsoft server products from 2010 onward (and in some cases even before then).

— **Snap-ins.** Snap-ins, or in proper PowerShell terminology, PSSnapins, is basically a set of DLL files that have accompanying XML files containing configuration information and the text that displays when you ask for help via `Get-Help`. Snap-ins were part of the first release of PowerShell back in the mid-2000s, and you will see fewer of these types of extensions as time goes on, as Microsoft and third parties obsolesce them in favor of modules. But there are still a few snap-ins around, so they deserve some coverage in this book.

Modules

Modules are, at this point, far and away the most common type of PowerShell extensibility feature you will see. They are basically containers filled with all the information PowerShell needs to work with a given piece of hardware or software, including the commands, the libraries necessary to get those commands to work, the help text, and any configuration information that might be required. Modules were designed as the next coming-on snap-ins and exist to remedy a lot of the things that make snap-ins sort of unwieldy and difficult to consume and distribute.

PowerShell looks for modules in certain directories on your system. You place the modules in that directory, and that's it—PowerShell handles the rest. You don't have to register them or perform any other steps. There is a PowerShell variable called `PSModulePath` that contains the directories where PowerShell is going to look for modules on your system, and because there usually are multiple directories to search for modules in, each directory is separated by a semi-colon with no spaces. No quotes are required here. How can you, ahem, *get* the *content* of this variable?

```
Get-Content env:PSModulePath
```

You either put paths in this directory, or you add the directory where other modules reside on your system to this path entry, which you can find in the Windows Control Panel. If I were you, I would just move modules into one of the two default directories and worry about other things.

What is particularly nice about modules is that, since they are stored in defined locations that PowerShell knows about in advance, they can be discovered automatically by the shell. So you get the advantage of being able to look for commands and have the help for a bunch of commands in a namespace that may or may not have been explicitly loaded yet, because PowerShell knows to look in *all* of the modules, not just the ones it has actively loaded. This is how you get the benefit of tab completion and (at least in the Windows PowerShell Integrated Scripting Environment) IntelliSense without having to manually add a zillion modules to your session each and every time you want to run a command.

If you have a module stored somewhere else, which is something that happens rather frequently with third-party PowerShell modules, you can import the module manually into your session by specifying the full path to the module with the Import-Module command.

```
Import-Module  c:\powershell\modules\thirdparty\coffee-
maker\
```

Modules can also add providers, which will then allow you, as you know, to walk up and down the configuration structure for a piece of software (or hardware, I suppose). To see whether any new providers were added when you added a module to your session, you can use the standard Get-PSProvider command we talked about in the previous half of the chapter. You'll see a list of names, capabilities, and drives you can use with this new module.

Snap-ins

As I mentioned, snap-ins are the other type of extension into PowerShell. For PowerShell to be able to use a snap-in, it must be registered with the system; otherwise it doesn't know how to use it or even that a snap-in exists. You can get a list of snap-ins that your system knows about right now by using `Get-PSSnapin -registered` from the console prompt. (Remember also that if you had not known that command off the top of your head, you could have searched via wildcards with a command like `Get-Command -noun *snapin*` and read the help.)

Once a snap-in is registered, you then have to load it into your console session to be able to use the commands it includes. What command do you think adds a snap-in?

That's right, it's `Add-PSSnapin`.

Once you have added a snap-in, it would be useful to see what commands it makes available to you. What command can we use to see other available commands? `Get-Command` is the right answer there, but do you think there is a way to limit the results of `Get-Command` to show us only the commands a certain snap-in makes available? What might that way be?

```
Get-Command -pssnapin name-of-snapin
```

See, you probably guessed that, or would have after a couple of tries at the console prompt. You are getting the hang of this!

Snap-ins can also add providers, which will then allow you, as you know, to walk up and down the configuration structure for a piece of software (or hardware, I suppose). To see whether any new providers were added when you added a snap-in to your session, you can use the standard `Get-PSProvider` command we talked about in the previous half of the chapter. You'll see a list of names, capabilities, and drives you can use with this new snap-in.

Again, since snap-ins are pretty rare these days, that's all the coverage I'll spend on them in this book. If you have snap-in questions specific to a certain product or service, then Googling for answers probably will prove fruitful. That is because these snap-ins are old and very well documented, and there will be a lot of experience using them on the Internet at large. Module assistance is a little more hit-or-miss when you are searching for support, but assistance for classic snap-ins that you are likely to encounter is just a search or two away in most cases.

About Management Shells

When you install the on-premises versions of some server products, like Exchange Server 2010, 2013, or 2016; SharePoint Server 2010, 2013, or 2016; and SQL Server 2008, 2012, or later; you will notice that alongside the regular graphically-based management tools built on the Microsoft Management Console platform, Microsoft installs "Management Shells" for each of these products. You might think that to execute PowerShell commands relating to Exchange, you need to launch the Exchange Management Shell, or to do some maintenance to Share-Point from the command line, you need to launch the SharePoint Management Shell application. This is not true, except in one case.

Basically, these shells just load up modules into a preconfigured window so that you are ready to go. They might import a module or load a PowerShell snap-in (I will show you what both of those processes mean and look like later in this section), but they just do it for the sake of convenience and also to reduce support calls. It's easier for a support representative to tell someone to go load the Exchange Management Shell than it is to run PowerShell, import a module, add this to the profile, and so on.

Oh, and that one exception? It's SQL Server 2008 and its cousin, SQL Server 2008 R2, which uses a specially compiled and functioning version of PowerShell that *is* in fact the only way to run PowerShell for those SQL versions. I don't really do much with SQL Server, and at any rate SQL Server is out of the scope of this book, which is aimed at total beginners, so that's the last I'll talk about that restriction. For SQL Server 2012 and later, you can use regular old PowerShell as long as you import the modules into your regular PowerShell console session.

Your Profile: Your Favorite Snap-Ins and Modules, Automatically Loaded

We're all lazy, right? No? Just me? OK, then you can skip this section. But if you're secretly lazy and you just don't want to admit it publicly, then read on. Wouldn't it be nice if you had a bunch of, say, third-party modules that you worked with regularly that, for whatever reason, you didn't want to put in the PowerShell automatic path locations but, since you worked with them a lot, you wanted them automatically loaded? The trick is to create a profile script and put the commands to load those modules in that script. When the PowerShell console starts, it looks in a hard-coded location for a profile script that it will automatically run at the start of the session. So that's a great place to set up your environment and get the stuff you normally work with ready and waiting for you without any effort on your part.

There is some work to do upfront, though. Here's what you want to do.

1. Run `Export-Console c:\mypreferredconsole.psc` to export a list of snap-ins to a file (snap-ins only here; you'll do the work for modules that don't reside in one of the paths that PowerShell looks at in `PSModulePath` in a moment).

2. Create a shortcut, maybe on your desktop or, if you're at the head of the class, in the Start menu hierarchy. Make the target (the destination) of that shortcut `%windir%\system32\WindowsPowerShell\v1.0\powershell.exe -noexit -psconsolefile c:\mypreferredconsole.psc` and save it.

3. Create a profile script. You need to create within your My Documents folder a directory exactly named `WindowsPowerShell` and then within it create a text file called `profile.ps1` (again, it must be named exactly that). Inside that file, type in on one line apiece any `Import-Module` commands that you normally use for modules that are not in the path directories. Save and exit.

4. Load the PowerShell console and issue `Set-ExecutionPolicy RemoteSigned`, which allows some scripts to run on your computer that were generated locally—in other words, not from the Internet or an unknown source—without prompting for advanced security confirmation.

5. Close PowerShell.

6. Reopen PowerShell. PowerShell is hard coded to look for `Documents\WindowsPowerShell\profile.ps1` and run it if it can find the file. Your modules will load automatically and you'll be ready to go. Easy as pie.

Just don't forget to add any future modules to your profile script, just on a new line for each one, so that your profile stays up to date with the modules that you use the most.

The Last Word

As I mentioned, my goal for this chapter of *Learning PowerShell* was to show you another of the most important features of PowerShell: providers, modules, and snap-ins. You even got to dive in deep into the Registry with your beginner PowerShell skills and turn off an important feature in Windows 10. Well done, ladies and gentlemen! Onward!

Chapter 5
The Complete Beginner's Guide to Objects

Welcome to Chapter 5 of *Learning PowerShell*. Today we talk about objects. No, not your stapler, or the object of your affection. PowerShell objects tie in nicely with our study of the pipeline from Chapter 3 and also what we're covering in the next chapter.

Let's dive in!

What Is an Object?

When you hear the term "objects," it probably brings up that fear of development and programming again. That sinking feeling, deep in your stomach, like something is about to happen that is just completely over your head. Fear not, though: objects in PowerShell are pretty simple, although there is a *ton* you can do to make them more complex. But for a beginner, we do not have to dive too deeply into objects to find them useful.

In PowerShell, an *object* is simply a way to represent data. Data can be in a lot of forms: it can be a table full of records, or it can be a spreadsheet, or a text file, or a long set of numbers separated by commas. In one sense, all data is just that: data. But objects are a way for PowerShell to use, handle, and spit out data in ways that make future operations possible and easier.

Consider the example of simple plain text. That is the easiest place to start. What if you have, in a simple text file, a table of students, their ID numbers, and their final exam score and final overall grade in a course? It might look something like this:

```
First Name   Last Name    ID   Exam   Grade
----------   ---------    --   ----   -----
Jon          Smith        01   84     B
Phil         Jones        02   90     B
Eric         Howard       03   91     A-
Jason        Stewart      04   77     C
Bill         Griffith     05   60     B-
Sara         Humphrey     06   92     A
Megan        Morgan       07   99     A+
Ashley       Russell      08   89     B+
```

DOI 10.1515/9781501506673-005

```
Rachel      Beattie     09   0    F
Camille     Williams    10   79   C
```

That is easy enough to represent on the screen, right? You would simply say
`Get-Content grades.txt` and that would display in the PowerShell window. Look at Figure 5.1 for proof.

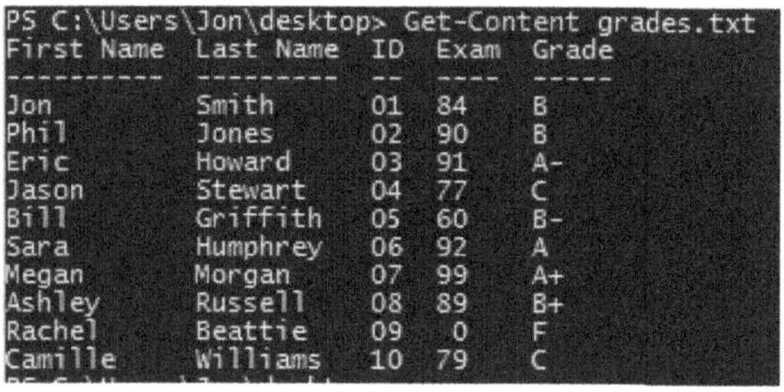

Figure 5.1: Displaying a text-based table in PowerShell.

Looking good. So, let's say then that I want to take advantage of the power of the PowerShell pipeline, and that I'd like to export that content to a CSV file so that I can then import it into Excel, Numbers, or whatever application I choose to use to manage numbers. I should be able to pipe that `Get-Content` command over to `Export-CSV` and then I should have a comma-separated values file ready for me, right? Let's try it.

`Get-Content grades.txt | Export-CSV grades.csv`

I run it, and it appears to go well, since as you can see in Figure 5.2, the command executes with no errors.

Figure 5.2: Running `Export-CSV` on a text file from `Get-Content`.

It even gives me a CSV file that appears on my desktop, since that's the folder from which I was running the command inside the PowerShell console window. You can see this in Figure 5.3.

grades

Figure 5.3: The resulting CSV file on my desktop.

So let's open it up! I did so, and my Excel window is shown in Figure 5.4.

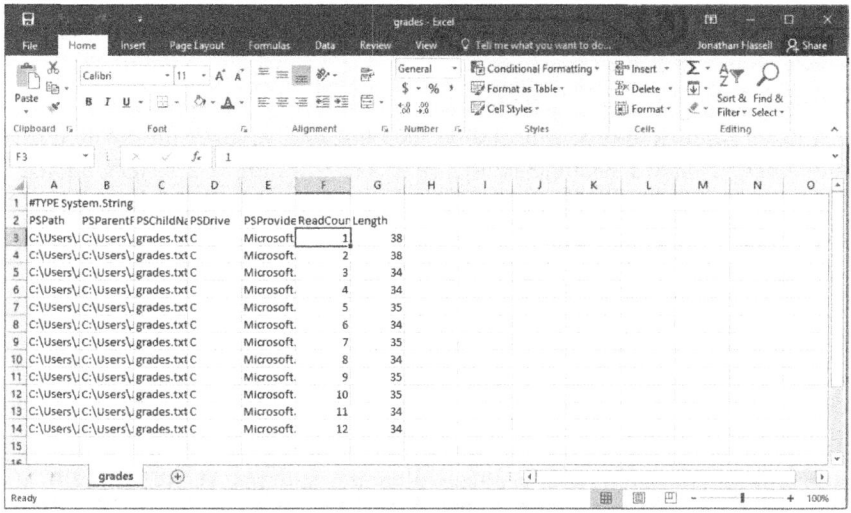

Figure 5.4: Opening the resulting CSV file in Excel.

What the hell is that?

Those are not my grades. Those are not my students, nor are those the ID numbers. What I have is a bunch of columns about PSPaths, PSParentPaths, read count, lengths, and other stuff. What happened to the table that PowerShell so neatly displayed when I ran Get-Content? Why wasn't that table simply reformatted into a CSV file? Where did all of this other stuff come from?

The explanation is that plain text files are not objects per se, and the PowerShell pipeline deals with objects, not just text. Objects allow the columns, rows, and individual records within my original text table to be handled with grace and aplomb by future commands down the PowerShell pipeline.

Let me explore this a little bit more. You can think of objects as sort of digitizing something into a tiny database or spreadsheet. Objects in PowerShell are manipulated in memory, and the pipeline commands do further interaction and manipulation to them, way before you ever see something written out to disk or displayed on your console screen. When you run, say, `Get-EventLog -LogName Application -Newest 10`, you see a text table on your screen, but that text table is far more to PowerShell. It is actually a representation of that "digital spreadsheet" that PowerShell is using within its memory. That is why you can do nifty stuff like getting only the newest 10 records, or formatting that table, or getting its properties, or writing only certain columns out to a HTML file for later consumption, or anything else. It's because of that digital spreadsheet, and that digital spreadsheet is a collection of objects—a representation of data that PowerShell both knows how to deal with and can consume and output using all the tools, commands, and functions at its disposal.

In truth, most of the things PowerShell touches, whether information from an event log, a new Exchange mailbox, a process running on a system, an Active Directory user, or anything else, have a lot of information about them available to PowerShell. You saw that in the example toward the end of Chapter 3, when we ran

```
Get-Eventlog -LogName Application -Newest 5 | ConvertTo-
Html | Out-File newest5app.html
```

The resulting HTML file had a lot of columns. If you actually open that file in your web browser and scroll right, you'll see all of the columns. There is EventID, MachineName, Data, Index, Category, CategoryNumber, EntryType, Message Source, ReplacementStrings, InstanceId, TimeGenerated, TimeWritten, UserName, Site, and Container. That's all of the information available to PowerShell from that digital representation—that *object* of the `Get-EventLog` command. But if you just run `Get-EventLog -LogName Application -Newest 5` from the console prompt and leave off the HTML conversion and the writing to disk, you see only a very small subset of those columns, as you see in Figure 5.5.

```
PS C:\Users\Jon\desktop> Get-Eventlog -LogName Application -Newest 5

Index Time          EntryType   Source              InstanceID Message
----- ----          ---------   ------              ---------- -------
13095 Nov 18 11:56  Information Windows Error Rep...       1001 Fault bucket 124882908176, type 5...
13094 Nov 18 11:56  Information Windows Error Rep...       1001 Fault bucket 124843187431, type 5...
13093 Nov 18 11:56  Information Windows Error Rep...       1001 Fault bucket 124849160376, type 5...
13092 Nov 18 11:55  Information Windows Error Rep...       1001 Fault bucket , type 0...
13091 Nov 18 11:55  Information Windows Error Rep...       1001 Fault bucket , type 0...
```

Figure 5.5: The display only shows a subset of the information a PowerShell object represents.

Let's step back for a moment. Think of trying to open that list of grades, as a text file, inside Excel. Excel doesn't understand the plain text format. It understands rows and columns only. So if I managed to get Excel to display the list of grades, which I might not even be able to do from a plain text file, it surely would not automatically put each student in a row and each piece of information about those students in the right columns. I would need a separate tool to be able to massage that data. But since PowerShell creates in its mind and memory the equivalent of a comma-separated values file, if Excel were PowerShell in this instance, it would know how to place all of the information correctly. I could hide columns and just display ID numbers and exam scores if I wanted to post grades publicly. I could sort by the head of the class to see who had top marks and who was not quite as adept. I could sort by the exam score to see how much my curve would be. All of this I could do because the CSV is an object, a digital representation, and not just plain text. PowerShell knows about and understands the contents of objects because those objects have defined and very well known things about them. That's why PowerShell objects are so powerful.

So initially, the things to remember here are that:

− objects are simply ways to represent data digitally, as opposed to just something like that, so that it can be manipulated;

− PowerShell likes objects and in fact everything PowerShell puts out is indeed an object itself;

− PowerShell can access a lot more about stuff (because that "stuff" is an object) that you can see on the screen when you run a command;

− sometimes the real power in PowerShell comes from the stuff you can touch that you can't initially see running a command here and there.

See, that wasn't so bad, right?

Properties and Methods

I'm going to throw a little bit more terminology your way. Put that "digital spread-sheet" back in your mind for second. The rows (with the numbers—1, 2, 3, 4, and so on) are objects. So in my text example with the list of grades above, John Smith's information and scores would be an object, Phil Jones' information and scores would be an object, and so on, all the way down to the last entry. Each row of the "digital spreadsheet" is an object.

But one thing about objects is that there are lots of ways to describe them and the characteristics they have. For example, each row in our grade "digital spread-sheet" has a student's first name, last name, ID number, final exam score, and overall course grade. Those things describe attributes of the object and are called *properties*. You can think of properties as the columns in our text file or the "dig-ital spreadsheet" because they contain information that describes the data in the row (remember each row is an object).

But then there are also things you can do to each row of our "digital spread-sheet." Bear with me, because my analogy breaks down just a little here, but I can still make it work. In the list of grades, each student has a score and a grade. What are some things I could do to that data? I could round each student's grade up to the nearest letter. I could apply a curve to the final exam scores. I could change a student's ID number. I could add or remove a student from my class. These things I can do to that data, to each row, are called *methods*. This roughly translates into the verb part of PowerShell's verb-noun command construction; the verbs are the action, or methods, associated with our rows (objects).

Finally, we need a word that encompasses our digital spreadsheet. In PowerShell parlance, our digital spreadsheet—all the rows—is known as a *collection*. At our be-ginner level, there is not much more to say about collections, so I will leave it there.

A quick recap:
- A *collection* is like a big digital spreadsheet in memory, full of rows and col-umns.
- The rows are individual *objects* we can deal with.
- The colums are *properties*, or characteristics the rows have.
- The things you can do with the rows are an object's *methods*.

Objects and the Pipeline

Objects are most useful when viewed and manipulated in conjunction with the PowerShell pipeline. You should note that objects, and all the properties and methods for those objects, reside in the pipeline until *every one of the commands in the pipeline has run*. That does *not* mean every object is always available in the pipeline, because some commands transform some types of objects into other types of objects, and sometimes, especially when you start filtering and excluding objects from the pipeline using some intermediate techniques you will soon learn, there is no standard definition of an object that matches the content in the pipeline. In these cases, PowerShell sort of makes it up on the fly and creates what it calls a PSObject, which is an object with a bunch of weird stuff in it with which it doesn't know how to deal. We'll worry about this later.

If you take away one thing from this section, remember that *everything that PowerShell puts out, either on screen or in the pipeline, is an object*. Even the simple stuff is an object. Until it hits your screen or is written to disk, all the output of any PowerShell command is an object, and that object will have properties and methods.

Inspecting an Object's Properties and Methods

So if everything output-wise in PowerShell is an object, then how do we know what properties those objects have? How do we know what methods will work on those objects?

All of those properties and methods for any given object are its *members*, and of course there is, drumroll please, a cmdlet for looking at them. It is `Get-Member`, which generally receives objects from the pipeline so that it can examine them. That allows you to do something to produce an object and then pipe whatever that is over to `Get-Member`.

The help files for any given command do not tell you what kinds of objects, properties, and methods are available. The only way to tell is to use the `Get-Member` command, as I am demonstrating in this section.

For example, let's look at `Get-EventLog` and see what we have going on.

```
Get-EventLog | Get-Member
```

Try that now. PowerShell will prompt you for the name of the log you care about; just type in Application for now. The next thing you'll notice will be the seemingly endless scrolling. Or maybe you have a faster machine than I do, because I hit Ctrl-C after about a minute of scrolling. What was all of that, and why did PowerShell behave that way? Well, remember, since you can consider the Application event log a giant digital spreadsheet, and since PowerShell spits out objects, PowerShell was running `Get-Member` against every single entry in the Application event log. Because every "row" of that event log is an object, it has its own properties and methods, and PowerShell did what you asked, albeit very literally.

Let's trim it down some.

```
Get-EventLog -LogName Application -Newest 1 | Get-Member
```

You'll see what happens in Figure 5.6.

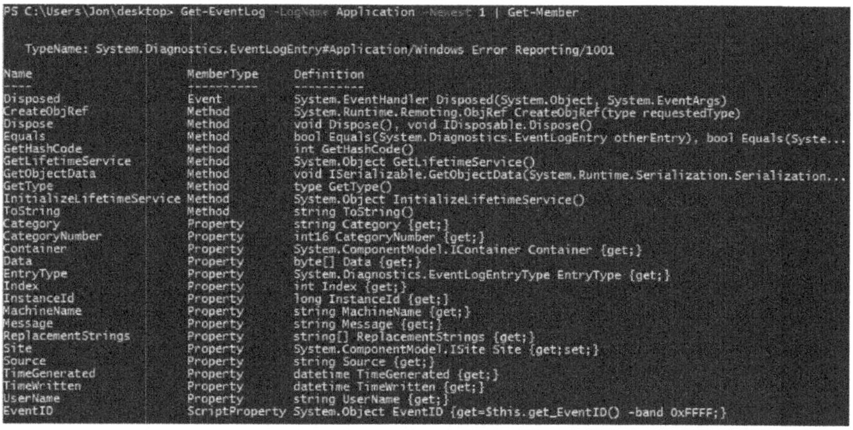

Figure 5.6: Showing the properties and methods of an event log entry object.

That's a lot nicer to look at, no?

In that, you can see that there are a few different member types—events (these are another type of member and refer to being able to do something once something else happens; don't worry about them for now), methods, properties, and an odd one out called `ScriptProperty`. Interestingly, `ScriptProperty` is still a property; it's just named differently because you can do some advanced stuff with it that we won't be getting into here in this beginning book. You can see there are methods that act like verbs—CreateObjRef, Dispose, Equals, a bunch of Gets, and more. You can see there are properties—Category, Container, Site, Source, EventID, and more—that you can easily imagine to be the column names in a spreadsheet. Is this all starting to make sense now?

In fact, what you are going to care most about with objects is their properties. Much of PowerShell is about reading something in about something, looking for something in command with a bunch of those things, doing something to those things that match your criteria, and then reading those things back out into a report or a confirmation message or some other type of output. Most of the time, an object's methods can be most easily accessed through regular old PowerShell commands—after all, they are built to work with object methods directly, and that's how they get things done. The properties—which again are like statuses or descriptions of states—are really where the meat of most administrative work lies.

Manipulating Objects

So now that you know that objects are lots of entries on giant digital spread-sheets, let's play a little with the format of the spreadsheets! When you're using PowerShell initially, you probably will want to do several things: get lists of stuff, like Active Directory users, event log entries, statistics about an Exchange public folder, and so on; and you'll want to hone in on just a few things you care about regarding each of those pieces. With PowerShell objects, you can sort by their properties, and you can also eliminate some properties from even displaying in output on the screen or in your disk-based output. Let's take a look.

Limiting or Selecting

Recall our earlier example in this chapter where we looked at the HTML output from the `Get-EventLog` command. There were several columns and, frankly, not all of them were interesting to us. A lot of them were there for programmatic reasons, but administrators probably are more interested in the event ID and the text of the event, and the date and time the event was written to the event log, rather than the rest of the stuff. So it would be nice to limit the output represen-tation of a PowerShell object to only the properties that we care about. What if we could *select* just the certain things about an *object* we were interested in seeing?

Well, we can, with the—you guessed it—`Select-Object` command. If we run a quick `Get-Help Select-Object`, we can see that the first parameter listed in the `-Property` parameter. Let's dig into an example here.

Remember that just running `Get-Command` naked, without any parame-ters, will list out every available PowerShell command on your system. It does so in a table format, with the table headers being CommandType, Name, Version, and Source. Those table headers in our "digital spreadsheet" are the properties, mind you. Let's say hypothetically that we don't care about the version of any command. We can use `Select-Object` to remove that column (which is really a property, remember), with the help of our old friend, the pipeline. What we will really do is select only the properties that interest us. That would be the CommandType property, which tells us if we're dealing with an alias, a function, a cmdlet, or otherwise, and the Name property, which has an obvious purpose. We do this by using the -Property parameter of Select-Object and then adding the properties one by one, with just a single comma and no spaces separating the entries.

```
Get-Command | Select-Object -property CommandType,Name
```

Run that now and see what happens. Your output trimmed, didn't it?

This is most useful when you want to pipe output to one of the ConvertTo or ExportTo commands, because instead of getting that giant brain dump of every conceivable thing about an object, you can get only the properties that are meaningful to you, making for much better reporting. Or maybe you're even writing to XML to ship data between business systems, so you want to limit the data stored in the XML to only what the destination system can accept and understand. This is one way to do that.

Sorting

Sorting is one way of doing organizing, and it's an incredibly useful one. Lots of times you want to know the top 5 of something, or the biggest or smallest something, and sorting is a quick way to get at that sort of information (see what I did there?).

We should probably start a new saying: There's a cmdlet for that! Because there is a cmdlet for sorting; it is called Sort-object. And with just a few exceptions, which generally would apply only in advanced scripting situations, Sort-object relies on the pipeline too. After all, Sort-object doesn't— well, it can't—do much if there isn't anything to sort.

Recall in Chapter 4 that I introduced to you the item set of commands, which you use when you are working with various providers and PSDrives to bounce up and down the "virtual disk" PowerShell creates for all of its different management structures. Let's use one of those item commands, Get-ChildItem, to actually do a simple directory listing. Here I will use the directory that includes all of the screenshots I am using within this book:

```
Get-ChildItem C:\Users\Jon\Dropbox\powershellforto-
talbeginners\manuscript\images
```

That returns a simple list of files, as shown in Figure 5.7.

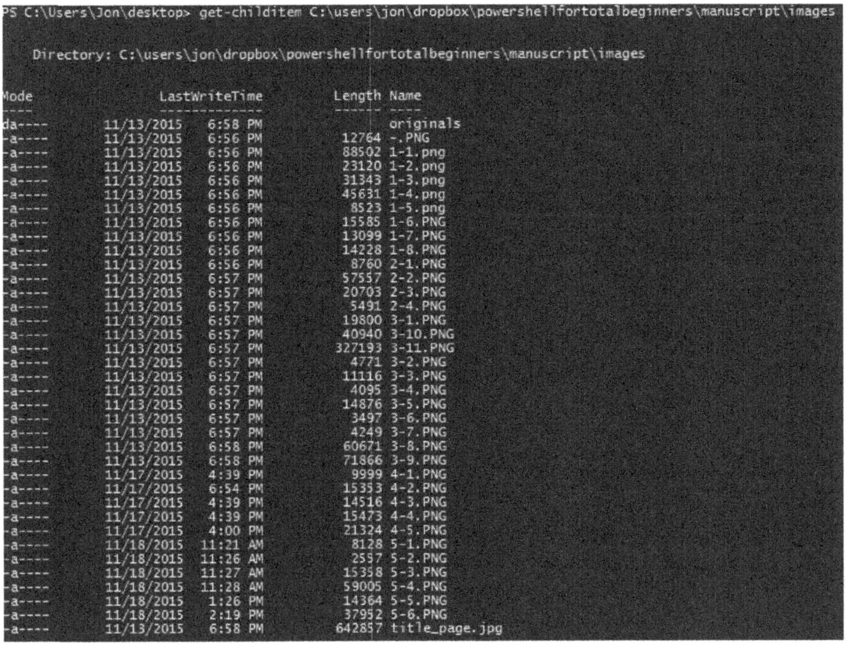

```
PS C:\Users\Jon\desktop> get-childitem C:\users\jon\dropbox\powershellfortotalbeginners\manuscript\images

    Directory: C:\users\jon\dropbox\powershellfortotalbeginners\manuscript\images

Mode                LastWriteTime         Length Name
----                -------------         ------ ----
da----       11/13/2015   6:58 PM                originals
-a----       11/13/2015   6:56 PM          12764 -.PNG
-a----       11/13/2015   6:56 PM          88502 1-1.png
-a----       11/13/2015   6:56 PM          23120 1-2.png
-a----       11/13/2015   6:56 PM          31343 1-3.png
-a----       11/13/2015   6:56 PM          45631 1-4.png
-a----       11/13/2015   6:56 PM           8523 1-5.png
-a----       11/13/2015   6:56 PM          15585 1-6.PNG
-a----       11/13/2015   6:56 PM          13099 1-7.PNG
-a----       11/13/2015   6:56 PM          14228 1-8.PNG
-a----       11/13/2015   6:56 PM           8760 2-1.PNG
-a----       11/13/2015   6:57 PM          57557 2-2.PNG
-a----       11/13/2015   6:57 PM          20703 2-3.PNG
-a----       11/13/2015   6:57 PM           5491 2-4.PNG
-a----       11/13/2015   6:57 PM          19800 3-1.PNG
-a----       11/13/2015   6:57 PM          40940 3-10.PNG
-a----       11/13/2015   6:57 PM         327193 3-11.PNG
-a----       11/13/2015   6:57 PM           4771 3-2.PNG
-a----       11/13/2015   6:57 PM          11116 3-3.PNG
-a----       11/13/2015   6:57 PM           4095 3-4.PNG
-a----       11/13/2015   6:57 PM          14876 3-5.PNG
-a----       11/13/2015   6:57 PM           3497 3-6.PNG
-a----       11/13/2015   6:57 PM           4249 3-7.PNG
-a----       11/13/2015   6:58 PM          60671 3-8.PNG
-a----       11/13/2015   6:58 PM          71866 3-9.PNG
-a----       11/17/2015   4:39 PM           9999 4-1.PNG
-a----       11/17/2015   6:54 PM          15353 4-2.PNG
-a----       11/17/2015   4:39 PM          14516 4-3.PNG
-a----       11/17/2015   4:39 PM          15473 4-4.PNG
-a----       11/17/2015   4:00 PM          21324 4-5.PNG
-a----       11/18/2015  11:21 AM           8128 5-1.PNG
-a----       11/18/2015  11:26 AM           2557 5-2.PNG
-a----       11/18/2015  11:27 AM          15358 5-3.PNG
-a----       11/18/2015  11:28 AM          59005 5-4.PNG
-a----       11/18/2015   1:26 PM          14364 5-5.PNG
-a----       11/18/2015   2:19 PM          37952 5-6.PNG
-a----       11/13/2015   6:58 PM         642857 title_page.jpg
```

Figure 5.7: Using `Get-ChildItem` to retrieve a directory listing.

You can see that those files appear to be sorted by name in ascending order. What if I care about finding the largest files instead? In that table, you can see the property name Length is how size is represented in PowerShell. In this case, the size of the file is referred to in PowerShell as the length of the file (kind of like the length of this book, in words, is in one way its size). So, we would use the pipeline to pipe the output of the `Get-ChildItem` command to `Sort-Object`. Let's do a quick `Show-Command Sort-Object` to what parameters there are that I might want to use; you can see this result in Figure 5.8.

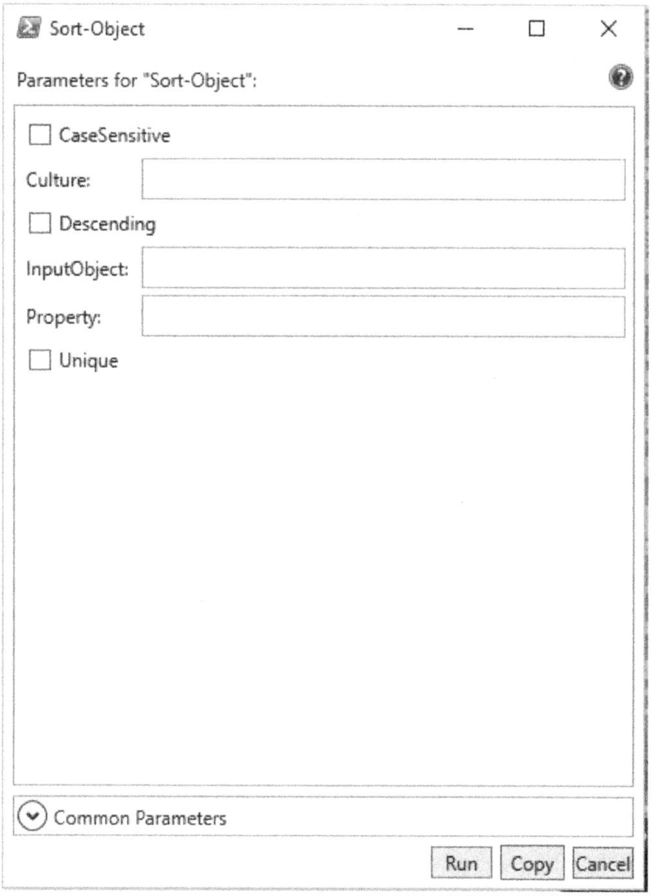

Figure 5.8: Checking out the parameters of `Sort-Object`.

Aha! There's Property, which as we know are the columns in the table. So I'll use:

```
Get-ChildItem    C:\Users\Jon\Dropbox\powershellforto-
talbeginners\manuscript\images | Sort-Object -property
Length
```

That results in what you see in Figure 5.9:

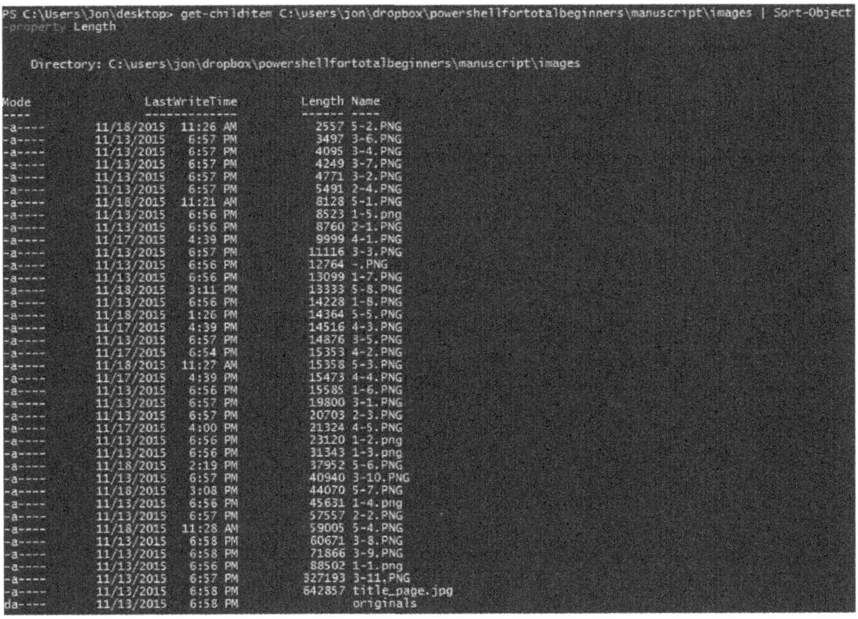

Figure 5.9: Trying out a sorting operation.

Interesting: it looks like the default sorting method is ascending, because we have the smallest files listed first and the largest files listed second. Now since there are not a ton of files in this directory, I can get the information I need from this command right as it stands—the file title_page.png is the biggest by far in this directory—but if I had a zillion files, the page would scroll and I would not get a sense of the distribution of the files. So let's see how we might sort in descending order, from largest at first to smallest last. Where could we do that? Oh, back in `Show-Command Sort-Object` we see there is a checkbox labeled "Descending." That must mean that descending order is a switch parameter. Let me add that to my command.

```
Get-ChildItem C:\Users\Jon\Dropbox\powershellforto-
talbeginners\manuscript\images | Sort-Object -property
Length -descending
```

Does that work?

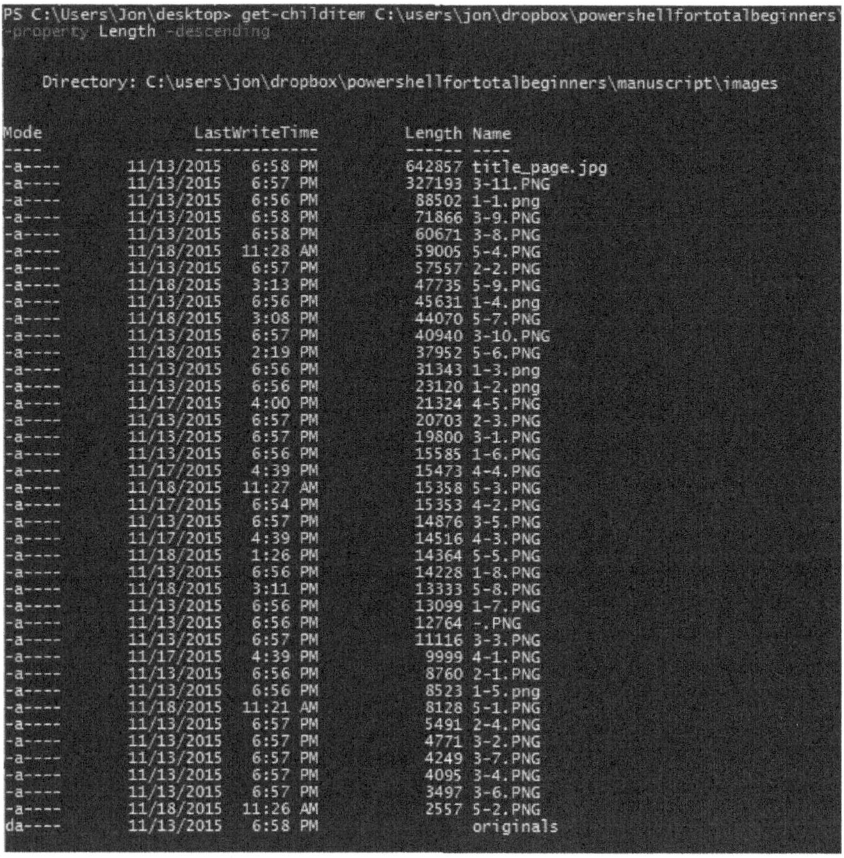

Figure 5.10: Trying out the `-descending` switch parameter for `Sort-Object`.

Yes! It does. That's my list in descending order.

Remembering What Kinds of Objects are in the Pipeline

Earlier in this chapter I mentioned that everything in the pipeline was an object, no matter how many commands you run, and everything in the pipeline remains an object until the last command is run. But I also discussed how sometimes the objects change based on what you want to do with them, and sometimes PowerShell simply makes up its own kind of object because you've filtered and sorted and selected your way to a set of properties and objects it doesn't know anything about.

This is a key bit to understand here when you start getting a little more advanced with your pipeline operations, because the output from one command is what the next command in the pipeline accepts. You may get to a point where one command far enough down in the pipeline can't understand the objects being piped to it because they have been transformed into something they don't know about or can't accept.

Follow my train of thought here. Let's use:

```
Get-EventLog -LogName Application -Newest 5
```

That produces a predictable result, by putting event log objects into the pipeline. You can tell this by piping to Get-Member and looking at the first line of the result output:

```
TypeName: System.Diagnostics.EventLogEntry
```

You don't have to worry now about the stuff after the pound sign. You can see EventLogEntry is the type of object that is output by that command.

So, let's pipe that into a Select-Object command so that we see only the EventID, Message, and TimeGenerated for those last five application event log entries.

```
Get-EventLog -LogName Application -Newest 5 | Select-Object -property EventID,Message,TimeGenerated
```

Now we've lopped off a bunch of members, so the object that is returned from the Select-Object command is different. Prove it to yourself by piping that last command further to Get-Member:

```
Get-EventLog -LogName Application -Newest 5 | Select-Object -property EventID,Message,TimeGenerated | Get-Member
```

You can see that has only seven members!

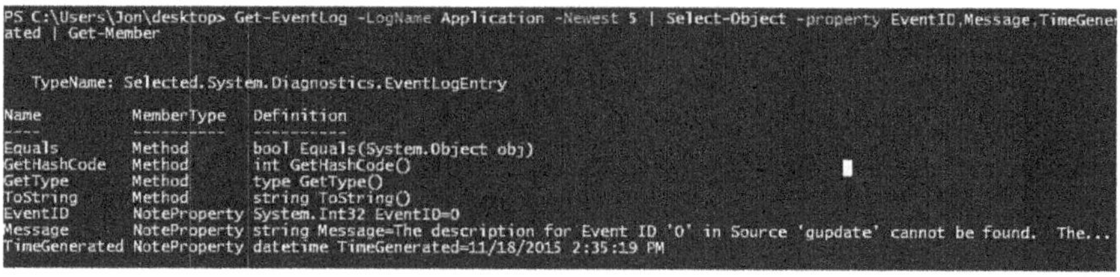

```
PS C:\Users\Jon\desktop> Get-EventLog -LogName Application -Newest 5 | Select-Object -property EventID,Message,TimeGene
ated | Get-Member

   TypeName: Selected.System.Diagnostics.EventLogEntry

Name          MemberType   Definition
----          ----------   ----------
Equals        Method       bool Equals(System.Object obj)
GetHashCode   Method       int GetHashCode()
GetType       Method       type GetType()
ToString      Method       string ToString()
EventID       NoteProperty System.Int32 EventID=0
Message       NoteProperty string Message=The description for Event ID '0' in Source 'gupdate' cannot be found.  The...
TimeGenerated NoteProperty datetime TimeGenerated=11/18/2015 2:35:19 PM
```

Figure 5.11: Examining a "PSObject."

The point here is that whatever the next command in pipeline is, it has to understand the type of objects it will receive from the previous command. It can be possible to start a pipeline that makes total sense, but after a bunch of filtering you end up with errors and you can't figure out why. That most likely has to do with the fact that some command somewhere in the pipeline has changed the type of object so much that the receiving command does not understand the input. This is an important troubleshooting step and one to remember. Sometimes you may need to unpack the pipeline a bit to diagnose where things are going wrong, and the Get-Member command will be a key tool in your arsenal for those diagnostics.

The Last Word

As I mentioned, my goal for this chapter of *Learning PowerShell* was to give you a sense of what objects are in the context of PowerShell and show why they make the pipeline so valuable and powerful. Onward!

Chapter 6
Filtering and Limiting

Welcome to Chapter 6 of *Learning PowerShell*. In Chapter 5, we learned all about objects, at least at a beginner's level. Objects are powerful differentiators that make PowerShell a rich and capable command-line environment. Understanding how to use objects and dig into their properties and methods unlocks the entire universe of PowerShell's abilities for you.

Most of the work you'll do with PowerShell, as I said in the previous chapter, involves looking at the properties of an object. But then you want to do something generally based on a specific property or two. For that, you need to be able to filter and limit. That's what this chapter is all about, PowerShell's built-in tools for filtering and limiting.

Let's dive in!

Introducing `Where-Object`

One of the most common uses of pipelining is to take the output of one cmdlet and filter it down into a certain subset of results; once you have filtered out the noise and you have your desired results, you then pipe that subresult set into another cmdlet to do some further magic.

This is where the `Where-Object` command comes in. `Where-Object` is one of the filtering mechanisms in PowerShell.

The Syntax for `Where-Object`

Now, the formatting of `Where-Object` gets a little funky, so stay with me while I show it to you. First off, you need to know some notations:

- { and } are curly brackets (in the same area as your backslash key, at least on US keyboards) and they denote logic. When you are making comparisons or setting up criteria for filtering, you enclose the criteria in curly brackets. It's kind of like the = sign in Excel that begins a formula, as in `=sum`, `=count`, `=average`, and so on.
- `$_` is shorthand for the current object. It's actually a little more complicated than that, but consider it to be the current object for the purposes of this chapter. Think of this in your head as whatever it is that you are working on. For example, the stuff (actually, the .NET object—remember from the last

DOI 10.1515/9781501506673-006

chapter that all PowerShell output is a .NET object) you get from the `Get-Process` cmdlet can be referred to in the pipeline next as `$_`.

- `-lt` is less than (i.e., 3 < 4, 3 is less than 4).
- `-le` is less than or equal to.
- `-gt` is greater than (i.e., 5 > 4, 5 is greater than 4).
- `-ge` is greater than or equal to.
- `-ne` is not equal to (i.e., 1 `-ne` 0, 1 is not equal to 0).
- `-like` is how you use text phrases for match words, phrases, and other text-based patterns.

That might feel a little down in the weeds, but the good news is that this syntax, this way of formatting, is found all over PowerShell. Learn it once and you'll be good to go and can use it everywhere.

Using the `Where-Object` Goods

To use the `Where-Object` cmdlet, you simply type in `Where-Object` and then a left curly brace, and then you start adding properties to compare with. You finish it off with a right curly brace so PowerShell knows that is the end of your query.

We spent last chapter talking about objects and how objects have members that are called properties, which are characteristics and descriptors about those objects. Now is a great time to use properties in a simple example about how `Where-Object` is really interesting.

Let's consider the `Get-Process` cmdlet, which, as you might expect, gets a list of the processes currently running on any given system. Give it a shot now on your test system; you do not need to include any parameters with it.
`Get-Process`

That output is shown in Figure 6.1.

```
Windows PowerShell
Copyright (C) 2014 Microsoft Corporation. All rights reserved.

PS C:\Users\jhassell> Get-Process

Handles  NPM(K)    PM(K)     WS(K) VM(M)    CPU(s)      Id ProcessName
-------  ------    -----     ----- -----    ------      -- -----------
    301      16     3224      3528   101      0.31    4272 AdobeARM
    190      12     2196      4240    94              2216 atieclxx
    129       7     1028      1260    31               836 atiesrxx
    164      11     6900      9876    40      0.23    2032 audiodg
    708      36    31080     65752   296      0.59    5212 Camera
   3280      94   122052      1528   963     94.64    1520 CCC
     68       8     1896      5820    58      0.03    3692 conhost
    294      12     1828      1912    48               432 csrss
    393      44     4124     15136   443               536 csrss
     66       6      960      2108    17              2156 dasHost
   1539     117   162080    169120   446  9,458.38    2128 Dropbox
    392      48    32872     41764   538               896 dwm
   2508     139   112608    178600   749    179.41     436 explorer
      0       0        0         4     0                 0 Idle
    800      57    22176     53844   313     47.56    2356 iexplore
    781     196   219872    250424   536    221.22    5168 iexplore
    874     702   651396    688292  1064  2,447.05    5180 iexplore
    150      10     1660      2124    46               440 igfxCUIService
    175      13     3360      4820   100      0.14    3164 igfxEM
   1284      27     9404     14044    50               584 lsass
    218      13     3348      9132   100      0.64    3736 mobsync
    360      36    27504      2892   602      1.08    4536 MOM
    600      61   110268    129904   461              1660 MsMpEng
   1146      33    84304    104436   260      2.80    4548 mstsc
    267      20    13880      4772    59              2152 NisSrv
     96       9     1488      7664    97      0.38    6020 notepad
    453      23    61380     62600   610      0.34    4628 powershell
    175      24    32196     11232   518              2472 PresentationFontCache
    821      77    55568     63456   650              3472 SearchIndexer
    255      11     5532      8260    35               576 services
    490      20     8892      9272   127     10.00    4564 SettingSyncHost
    661      31    27176     24628   212     45.92    3716 SkyDrive
   1766     193   122612    117868   608    971.78    4936 Skype
     44       2      276       332     4               312 smss
    422      27     5532      7464    81              1268 spoolsv
    493      20     7128     11344    62               664 svchost
    483      18     5804      7796    45               756 svchost
    818      28    19196     20484   103               880 svchost
    791      30    29992     36244   126               912 svchost
   2083     104    57612     65668   745               948 svchost
    686      37    14124     19996   117               980 svchost
    995      48    15924     17904  1420              1040 svchost
    480      38    19688     18756   109              1296 svchost
    389      18     6908     12528   118              1440 svchost
     54       6      696      1096    21              1468 svchost
     51       6      684      1084    21              1500 svchost
    145      11     1928      2400    42              1636 svchost
    353      20     5264     11204    83              3244 svchost
    954       0      128     10424    16                 4 System
    344      25     6028     10772   496     10.73    2304 taskhostex
    136      11     2720      7460    62               764 TiWorker
     96       8     1576      4668    30              2136 TrustedInstaller
     76       8      796       608    44               528 wininit
    165       9     1704      2712    59               700 winlogon
    177      13     3316      7936    41              5240 WmiPrvSE
```

Figure 6.1: The Get-Process command.

Let's say we want to find all processes that used more than 1,000 seconds on all the processors in the system. This can indicate a long-running process, or a process that's gone out of control, or something else. We'll use Where-Object to do the filtering, and `Get-Process` to get all the initial process information from which we'll do our filtering. So in the PowerShell window, we'd type:

```
Get-Process | Where-Object { $_.
```

Now what do we type next? This is a great time to recall and remember and use the tab-ahead feature of the PowerShell window. You'll remember from Chapter 1 of this very book you hold in your electronic hands right now that tab ahead lets you press the Tab key to cycle through all the possible valid entries for whatever you're typing. Right now, since we just entered the period, PowerShell is going to let us cycle through all the available property names that we'd like to use. This is an incredibly valuable feature if you don't know exactly what you're looking for. Additionally, if you kind of know what you're looking for, it'll help you pinpoint it.

Here, since we know we're after CPU times, we can type in `CP` and press Tab and we'll see the PowerShell window add in the `U` for us, completing the identification.

```
Get-Process | Where-Object { $_.CPU
```

Time to build the actual comparison logic. We want everything greater than or equal to (so we'd use the `ge` tag) 1,000 CPU seconds. That will look like this:

```
-ge 1000
```

So now, we have built:

```
Get-Process | Where-Object { $_.CPU -ge 1000
```

And since we have completed building our "where" clause, we just add the right curly brace to finalize things and finish off our comparison statement.

```
Get-Process | Where-Object { $_.CPU -ge 1000 }
```

Run that at your console window, and see what happens.

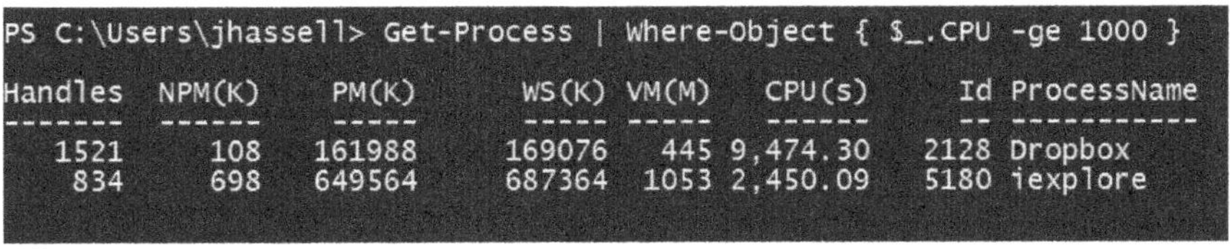

```
PS C:\Users\jhassell> Get-Process | Where-Object { $_.CPU -ge 1000 }

Handles  NPM(K)    PM(K)     WS(K) VM(M)   CPU(s)      Id ProcessName
-------  ------    -----     ----- -----   ------      -- -----------
   1521     108   161988    169076   445 9,474.30    2128 Dropbox
    834     698   649564    687364  1053 2,450.09    5180 iexplore
```

Figure 6.2: The Get-Process | Where-Object { $_.CPU -ge 1000 } command.

Hark! A list of the two processes that have CPU seconds over 1000. Guess who the culprit is here? Looks like Dropbox has been running a long time on this system, which is true, given it has been up without a reboot for several weeks and I use Dropbox constantly (and it runs in the background synchronizing files, too).

What's pretty cool is that within your comparison logic, you can use the and parameter to add another set of criteria. For instance, in the above example, we could add another criterion that says we want the list to be filtered not only on CPU time, as we discussed, but also on the number of handles. More specifically, we want all processes that meet the CPU time criteria and have handles greater than 1,000.

See if you can build that clause yourself now, without looking ahead. We're six chapters into this book, so you should have enough self-confidence to take a stab at it. Go for it! I'll go get a cup of coffee.

Finished? That clause would look like this:

```
Get-Process | Where-Object { $_.CPU -ge 1000 -and
$_.Handles -ge 1000 }
```

See how that works? You can keep going on and on and on, but obviously at some point your filter becomes really tight. But that's how you add criteria to Where-Object and how you construct the comparison clauses.

Getting Lists and Filtering on Them

In this section, we'll return to an old friend: Get-ChildItem.

As you know, at its core, Get-ChildItem exists to get information on all of the things stored within something. If that something is the parent, the things stored within it are child items, and thus the name of the cmdlet was born. For example, a folder contains files, so when we point Get-ChildItem at a folder, what do you think we'd get back? Let's take a look in Figure 6.2.

```
PS C:\Users\jhassell> Get-ChildItem c:\windows

    Directory: C:\Windows

Mode                LastWriteTime    Length Name
----                -------------    ------ ----
d----         8/22/2013  11:36 AM           addins
d----         8/22/2013  11:36 AM           ADFS
d----        10/11/2015   1:06 AM           AppCompat
d----        10/10/2015   5:01 PM           apppatch
d----        11/20/2015   8:18 AM           AppReadiness
d-r--        10/15/2015   4:16 AM           assembly
d----         8/22/2013  11:36 AM           Boot
d----         8/22/2013  11:36 AM           Branding
d----        11/21/2014  11:17 AM           Camera
d----        10/14/2015   8:01 AM           CbsTemp
d----        10/10/2015   3:29 PM           CSC
d----         8/22/2013  11:36 AM           Cursors
d----        10/10/2015   4:07 PM           debug
d-r--         8/22/2013  11:36 AM           DesktopTileResources
d----         8/22/2013  11:36 AM           diagnostics
d----         8/22/2013  11:43 AM           DigitalLocker
d---s         8/22/2013  11:36 AM           Downloaded Program Files
d----        11/21/2014  11:16 AM           en-US
d----        11/21/2014  11:17 AM           FileManager
d-r-s        10/14/2015   8:01 AM           Fonts
d----         8/22/2013  11:36 AM           Globalization
d----        11/21/2014   3:00 AM           Help
d----        11/21/2014  11:17 AM           IME
d-r--        10/10/2015   5:01 PM           ImmersiveControlPanel
d----        11/13/2015   4:47 PM           Inf
d----         8/22/2013  11:36 AM           InputMethod
d----         8/22/2013  11:36 AM           L2Schemas
d----         8/22/2013  11:36 AM           LiveKernelReports
d----        10/17/2015   3:00 AM           Logs
d-r-s         8/22/2013  11:36 AM           Media
d----        11/21/2014  11:17 AM           MediaViewer
d----        11/20/2015   3:55 AM           Microsoft.NET
d----        10/10/2015   3:45 PM           Migration
d----         8/22/2013  11:36 AM           ModemLogs
d-r--         8/22/2013  11:36 AM           Offline Web Pages
d----        10/11/2015   8:46 AM           Panther
d----        10/10/2015   5:10 PM           PCHEALTH
d----         8/22/2013  11:36 AM           Performance
d----         8/22/2013  11:36 AM           PLA
d----        10/10/2015   5:01 PM           PolicyDefinitions
d----        11/20/2015   1:01 AM           Prefetch
d----         8/22/2013  11:36 AM           Registration
d----        10/16/2015   3:46 AM           rescache
d----         8/22/2013  11:36 AM           Resources
d----         8/22/2013  11:36 AM           SchCache
d----         8/22/2013  11:36 AM           schemas
d----        11/21/2014   3:25 AM           security
d----         8/22/2013  10:45 AM           ServiceProfiles
d----        11/21/2014  11:17 AM           servicing
d----         8/22/2013  10:45 AM           Setup
d----        10/10/2015   5:11 PM           ShellNew
d----        11/21/2014   3:25 AM           SKB
d----        10/10/2015   3:48 PM           SoftwareDistribution
d----         8/22/2013  11:36 AM           Speech
d----         8/22/2013  11:36 AM           System
d-r--        11/17/2015   4:02 PM           System32
d----         8/22/2013  11:36 AM           SystemResources
d----        11/13/2015   4:44 PM           SysWOW64
d----         8/22/2013  11:36 AM           TAPI
d----        10/11/2015   9:38 AM           Tasks
d----        11/20/2015   9:43 AM           Temp
d-r--        10/10/2015   5:01 PM           ToastData
d----         8/22/2013  11:36 AM           tracing
d----        11/21/2014  11:17 AM           twain_32
d----         8/22/2013  11:36 AM           vpnplugins
d----         8/22/2013  11:36 AM           vss
d----         8/22/2013  11:36 AM           Web
d----        10/10/2015   5:01 PM           WinStore
d----        10/14/2015   8:01 AM           WinSxS
```

Figure 6.3: The Get-ChildItem command pointed at a target folder.

But Get-ChildItem is also capable of going up through subdirectories or subfolders (or down through them, depending on your point of view) and getting information about the child items within the folders of the original child items. This is called *recursion*, and you can enable this parameter simply by including -recurse in your command. For example, try this on for size in your own copy of PowerShell:

```
Get-ChildItem c:\windows -recurse
```

On my brand-new Core i5 machine at 2.9 GHz with 32 GB of RAM and a solid-state hard drive, that command took a few minutes (!) to run. That's because it's enumerating every single file within the Windows folder, even if those files are deeper within subfolders under C:. With one command. It would take you a lot more mouse clicks to get through the Windows Explorer GUI to do the same thing.

Are you beginning to see why they call it *Power*Shell?

Filtering, in a Pragmatic Sense

So let us use our newfound power for good and not for amusement. Let's say we have a server. Its main hard drive or storage array or default volume, or whatever you want to call it, is filling up. You suspect that some of your users are storing giant video files on this volume, and you want to find out if this is true. How could we find out in PowerShell?

Let's assume we're looking for files with the .mp4 extension, as that's probably the most commonly used file. (In reality, you could search for any extension you wish, but this is a pretty decent example.) We want to find the video files in c:\users because our users don't have access to any other part of the disk; that is the root of their home directories shared out through SMB and mapped through Group Policy. That's a pretty standard setup you get out of the box in most Windows deployments if you are using folder redirection.

So we tell PowerShell we want information about files in C:\Users in this way:

```
Get-ChildItem c:\users -recurse
```

Now how do we search for the extensions? Remember, Get-ChildItem is going to return all of the information about the files, which would be information overload for our purposes. Let's jog our memories. What command do we use to filter out information? Oh yeah, `Where-Object`. And how do we get things to `Where-Object`? Of course: the pipeline!

```
Get-ChildItem c:\users -recurse | Where-Object
```

Ah, we need the comparison logic now. We'll add the left curly brace (`{`) to begin the comparison expression, include the "that thing" notation (`$_`), and the period to access the properties of the .NET object that results from the `Get-ChildItem` cmdlet.

```
Get-ChildItem c:\users -recurse | Where-Object { $_.
```

Hmm. We're looking for extensions, so I'll type in `Ext` and see what comes up by tabbing through the options.

```
Get-ChildItem c:\users -recurse | Where-Object { $_.Extension
```

`-Extension` is one of them! There we go. So now I want the extension to equal `.mp4`, so I'll use the `eq` comparison (remember the list above) and then enclose `.mp4` in quotes because, well, take my word for it for now: when you're searching for text and not numbers, enclose the text in quotes.

```
Get-ChildItem c:\users -recurse | Where-Object { $_.Extension -eq ".mp4"
```

Now just add the right curly brace and we are off to the races.

```
Get-ChildItem c:\users -recurse | Where-Object { $_.Extension -eq ".mp4" }
```

Figure 6.4 shows what I get back.

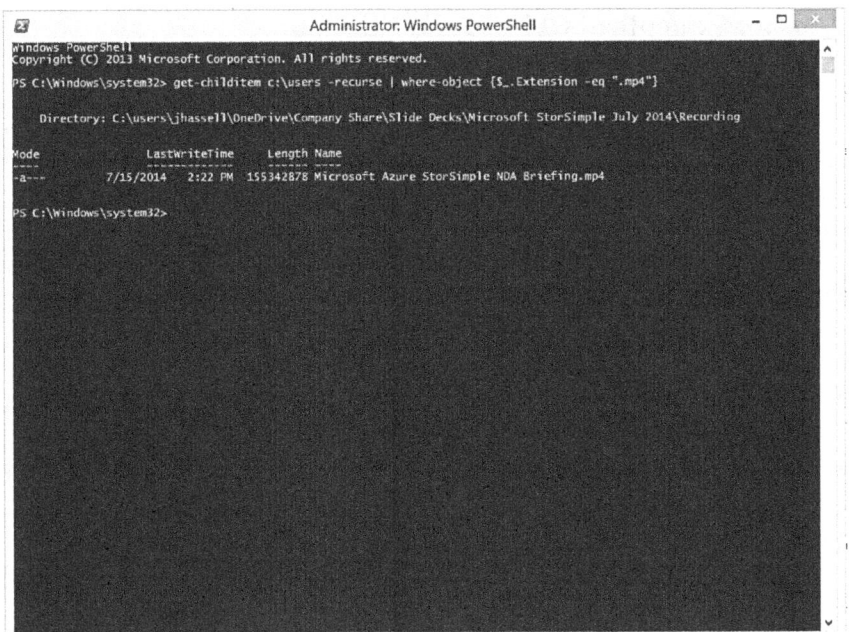

Figure 6.4: Searching for video and audio files in a target folder.

Voila! Now I don't have many video files on this system—just one—but if I ran this on my server, it would come back with quite a few. And other extensions would of course return different results. But now you know how to figure this sort of file management out with PowerShell and not with a billion right-clicks and shift-clicks inside the GUI.

Now some of you might get an error. This is probably because you are not running your Windows PowerShell instance as an administrator. Recall that we talked about this in Chapter 1; this is one of those instances when you are doing something that requires you to elevate yourself to an administrator account to carry out your intended action. Essentially, the reason why you need to run as an administrator is that when you search C:\Users, PowerShell can access only the parts of C: that your current user account has permission to access. By running as an administrator, you can generally search all of C:\Users.

Another Example of Objects and Filtering

Let's use another example, if for no other reason than to really hit the points home. Hypothetically, let's say you have been infected with Cryptolocker on one of your business' machines. This is a nasty ransomware bug; it is malware that silently encrypts the files it finds in a couple of places on your machine (My Documents and mapped drives being a couple of them). And then the bug makes you pay several hundred dollars in untraceable Bitcoin or Green Dot prepaid debit cards to get the key to decrypt them. You either pay up or you lose access to your files.

In our example, let's assume you were able to find the infection before it had the time to encrypt all your files. You immediately shut down the machine, so the encryption process stopped, but as part of your diagnosis of what happened, you need to figure out a list of all the files modified in the past day or so. Here we can again use `Get-ChildItem`, your tool of choice when you want to grab something out of a giant container of items—in this case the file system.

We know to start with `Get-ChildItem`, but how do we know what parameters to put along with it?

First, we can check out `Get-Help Get-ChildItem`, which will show us that the syntax starts off with `-Path`. We know that if we are concerned with potentially encrypted data at the mapped drive S: where shared documents are stored, we would use `-Path S:\` to establish where to look.

But what about subdirectories, subfolders, and any sort of nested structure we want to examine as well? From `Get-Help Get-ChildItem`, we also see the `-Recurse` parameter; as you now know, recursive checking means the program will start at the top and then "recurse," or walk down, the hierarchy of files until everything has been properly examined. We'll add that to the cmdlet as well.

That brings us to this partial cmdlet:

```
Get-ChildItem -Path S:\ -Recurse
```

You can actually run that, and PowerShell will spit out a list of every single file on the S: volume separated out by subdirectory. But we need to examine more about that huge list of files, so we will use the pipeline function to send that output into another cmdlet.

But what cmdlet helps us select a portion of a big set of data for further processing? Recall now that that function is the job of the `Where-Object` cmdlet.

So our cmdlet takes on further shape and body:

```
Get-ChildItem -Path S:\ -Recurse | Where-Object
```

Remember that we add in curly braces, and then within them we can use the $_,
or as I like to affectionately call it, "that thing," to represent the output of a previous cmdlet being piped into a new cmdlet. Then, we add a period or dot and
then the name of a property of that object represented by $_.

Here is what we have so far:

```
Get-ChildItem -Path S:\ -Recurse | Where-Object {$_.
```

But what is Where-Object going to filter? That's where we need to find out
what the properties of Get-ChildItem are; we can use those properties to
"tune the antenna," so to speak, of Where-Object so that it is filtering on the
right criteria. Do you remember how to find the properties that can be filtered of
any given object?

To find those properties, let us consult with Get-Member, which you
learned about in Chapter 5. As a quick refresher, we know we need to use the
command we're interested in and then pipe the output of that command to Get-
Member so that it can properly examine the types of objects and their members
that that given command puts out. So we'll use:

```
Get-ChildItem | Get-Member
```

And Figure 6.5 shows the results of that command on my system.

Figure 6.5: Finding the properties of `Get-ChildItem` we can use.

Looking at that result, I can see two properties that might be interesting to us for completing our task: `LastWriteTime` and `LastWriteTimeUtc`. This is what we're looking for! We need the last time that a file was written to.

In this case, just to make things simple, we will use `LastWriteTime` rather than worrying about converting time zones to Greenwich Median Time, although you might have a specific purpose for doing so as you progress in your scripting capabilities.

So to put together our fuller picture, here is where we are:

```
Get-ChildItem  -Path  S:\  -Recurse  |  Where-Object
{$_.LastWriteTime
```

So we have identified the last write time, but we obviously need to do something with that; we need to ask ourselves, in constructing this command, the question: "Where the last write time is *what*, exactly?" So we need a comparison operator.

We learned in the first section of this chapter that we can use -lt for "less than" and -gt for "greater than." So in order to figure out what was written in the last day or so, we can pick a date two days ago. In this example, today is May 14, 2015, so if I'm trying to figure out what files have been touched in the past 24 hours, I would want to know files where the last write time is greater than May 12, 2015.

We write this out in standard MM/DD/YYYY format and then enclose it in quotes, as it is considered a string. Then we will add the closing curly brace because our comparative clause is complete, and we have the following cmdlet built:

```
Get-ChildItem -Path S:\ -Recurse | Where-Object
{$_.LastWriteTime -gt "05/12/2015"}
```

Run that, and you will get a list of every file on the S: volume that has been written to on 5/12/2015 or after—exactly what we were looking for. And we did that by understanding that

- (a) the output of Get-ChildItem is an object, and
- (b) we can find the properties of the Get-ChildItem output object using Get-Member and use those properties to
- (c) pipe to Where-Object to find specific information about a subset of that output.

Further Exploration

There are all sorts of convenient ways to use objects and their properties and methods. With all output being an object, it means you can sort and filter all sorts of attributes and characteristics of whatever it is you are working on.

For instance, you can display information in a table format that eliminates all the other facts you have no interest in and laser-focuses on facts you are interested in. For example, let's look at what is available for Get-Service.

```
Get-Service | Get-Member
```

If I run that, I will see in the resulting table that Status is a property and Start and Stop are methods. So if I wanted to find out all the services on a machine that were in the Stopped state, and start those services, I might want to build the following cmdlet:

```
Get-Service | Where-Object {$_.Status -eq "Stopped"} |
Start-Process
```

Or consider a different scenario with different software. What if I wanted to find all of the Exchange mailboxes that had been created in my lab Exchange environment and then delete those mailboxes because I am done with my experiment and want to restore my test deployment? First, I would want to see the properties available for the Get-Mailbox cmdlet, a core cmdlet of Exchange or Office 365:

```
Get-Mailbox | Get-Member
```

I would see, among dozens of other properties, the WhenChanged property. This might work, so I would test this out:

```
Get-Mailbox | Format-List name,WhenChanged
```

This gives me a list of mailboxes with the mailbox-friendly name and the value of the WhenChanged property. Looks like what I need, so I will modify the above cmdlet not to display a list, but to receive the output of Get-Mailbox into a Where-Object filter, where I will grab the WhenChanged output and pass, for deletion, only those that meet my comparison criteria via the pipeline to the Remove-Mailbox cmdlet. It ends up looking like this:

```
Get-Mailbox | Where-Object {$._WhenChanged -gt
"05/07/2015"} | Remove-Mailbox
```

Voila.

The Last Word

As I mentioned, my goal for this chapter of *Learning PowerShell* was to show you PowerShell's built-in tools for filtering and limiting. Now in the next chapter, we'll put objects, filtering, and limiting together and make some simple scripts.

Onward!

Chapter 7
Creating Simple Scripts

Welcome to Chapter 7 of *Learning PowerShell!* In this chapter, I am going to get loopy. But before we do that, it's crucial for us to learn how to put together some simple scripts. Once we have the framework of creating our own scripts down, we can add in some of the more advanced logic that involves loops and conditionals.

Let's get started!

Introducing Scripts in PowerShell

Scripts in PowerShell are basically just text files with a special filename extension, ps1. To create a script, you would enter a bunch of PowerShell commands in a sequence in a new Notepad file (or you could use any text editor you like), and then save that file as `NAME.ps1`, where NAME is a friendly description of your script—with no spaces, of course.

To run a PowerShell script you already have, you either enter at a PowerShell window:

- the full path (folder and file name) of the script, like `c:\powershell\myscripthere.ps1`

or

- if your script is in the current directory the console is looking at, a period and then a backslash, like `.\myscripthere.ps1`

Other than that, there is nothing special to creating a script in PowerShell. You simply add the commands you like.

Of course, a script probably needs to do more than one thing or you wouldn't need a script for it. Scripts are common in IT; administrators have been using login scripts for decades to get users' desktops and environments configured consistently every time a user logs on. As technology has gotten better, you can script almost anything, even the bare metal installation of an operating system on a server fresh out of the factory box all the way up to the server workloads running. We obviously won't go that in depth in this beginner's book, but the basic idea behind a script for our purposes is to do two or three things and then end.

To do that, we need to cover a few elements of a script. The first is the element that can change. The second is the element of the script that does the dirty work on everything. Let's look at each of the phases.

DOI 10.1515/9781501506673-007

Making Scripts Useful, Phase 1: Variables

Now if you buy that the whole point of scripting is to do things over and over again in a consistent way, then you have to buy the idea that you want to do the same action to different things. But how do you change the things that are being acted upon? *Variables* are how. Variables are kind of like holders, and you can put values, words, numbers, basically anything within them. In PowerShell, variables always have a dollar sign ($) before them.

Let me declare a few variables for you right now.

```
$name = Jon
$number = 12345
$location = Charlotte
$listofnumbers = 6,7,8,9
$my_last_math_grade = D+
```

All I had to do to declare (in other words, to set up for the first time) those variables was add a dollar sign, then whatever name for the variable I wanted—no spaces are allowed—and then a space, an equals sign, another space, and whatever I wanted the value of the variable to be. If I want to have a variable with text as its value, I need to add a single quote on either side of the text. (There are some exceptions to this, but again my goal here is to keep it simple so we'll stick with this for now.) You also can just declare a variable without putting a value in it. This kind of reserves the name, which is probably more helpful when you're in the middle of developing than at any other time.

You know what else you can put in a variable? The output of a cmdlet. Throughout this book, we've been using the simple example of looking at the most recent five events in the Application event log, and you'll recall the command for that is:

```
Get-EventLog -LogName Application -Newest 5
```

But you can make that command store its output in a variable by declaring a variable exactly the way I just showed you, and then using the command name in full after the = sign. Like this:

```
$newapplicationlogevents = Get-EventLog -LogName Appli-
cation -Newest 5
```

Type that in at a prompt and press Enter. You won't receive any feedback because you've directed the output of the command into the variable that you declared. But, as with any variable, you can check its value at any time from the command prompt just by entering the name of the variable, with nothing else, and pressing Enter.

```
$newapplicationlogevents
```

In this case, as you can see from Figure 7.1, PowerShell returns the output of the command at the time it was run.

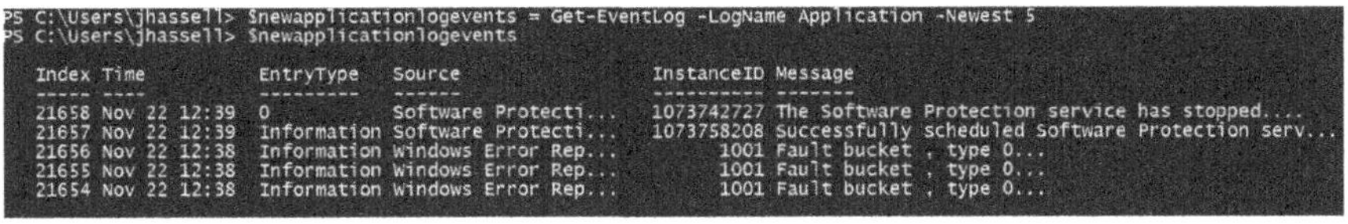

Figure 7.1: Declaring a variable, and putting the output of a command in it.

Success! Now you can use that variable as part of something else. For a simple example, let's look at the `Write-Host` cmdlet, which, as you might remember, simply writes text to the screen of the machine hosting the PowerShell session. `Write-Host` has a bunch of capabilities—do you remember how to use `Get-Help` to find out what those are if you're curious?—but in its simplest form, you can just say:

```
Write-Host "Whatever text I want, as long as it is inside
double quotes."
```

Seriously, you can cut and paste that line into a PowerShell window and it'll come out exactly as it goes in. If you don't believe me, just try it.

But what you can do is integrate variables with `Write-Host`. You just call them with the dollar sign notation and work them right into your text. Let me teach you a trick for now. Recall the command `Get-Command`? Well for most commands, if you want to count the discrete number of objects returned in the collection, you can simply enclose the command in parentheses and then use a period (.) and the property `count` to get the quantity. So, if we used `Get-Command` to list out all the commands available on our system, we could just get the count by using

```
(Get-Command).count
```

Do that now and see what happens. On my system, it looks like what you see in Figure 7.2.

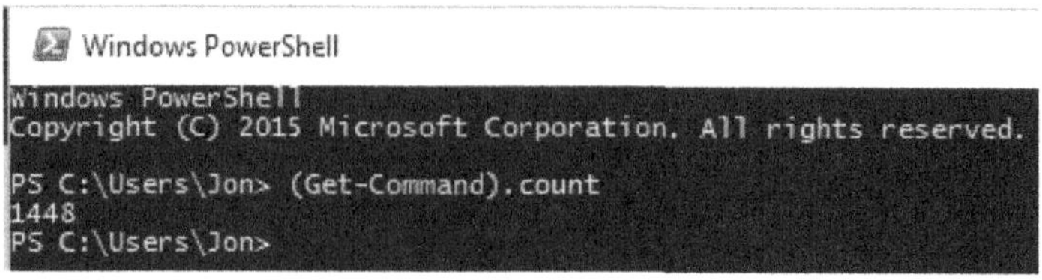

Figure 7.2: Getting the count of commands.

Let's then declare a variable and place that count inside the variable's value.
```
$numberofcommands = (Get-Command).count
```

Then, we can use `Write-Host` to work that value into a regular sentence that would be output right to the console screen.

For example, I can say:

```
Write-Host "There are $numberofcommands commands
available for use on this system."
```

And what does PowerShell return to us? Take a look in Figure 7.3.

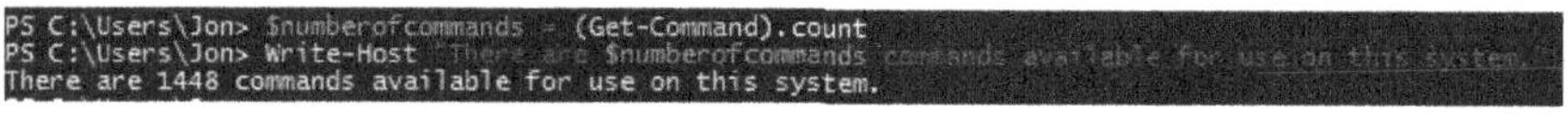

Figure 7.3: Using `Write-Host` to write out the value of a variable.

It's almost as if we meant for that to happen!

Let's put a pin there in variables for now, and move on to the next element of scripting: decision making and looping.

Making Scripts Useful, Phase 2: If/Then, Do While, and ForEach

The next phase is to actually do some magic. We know how to store values in variables now, but we need to do some things to those variables. Let's take a look.

The If/Then Construct

The simplest form of decision making in PowerShell is the if/then mechanism in PowerShell lingo. This is called the construct and it basically works like this:

If something is some comparison to something else

--> Then do this action

You format it by putting your comparison in parentheses, putting a left curly brace alone on a new line, adding the PowerShell commands or actions to perform if that action is true on another new line, and then ending with a right curly brace on a final new line. The key parts here are that:

— the comparison statement must have a logical response of either TRUE or FALSE. Think of it as a yes or no question. If you need to do something not based on a yes or no question, then another loop construct is appropriate; we'll cover that in a bit.

— the code that runs if your statement is YES or NO must be within curly braces, and it is best practice to put these curly braces on lines by themselves so that you can match them up when you are writing more complicated scripts.

For example, if I wanted to compare two numbers—let's say 5 and 10—and have PowerShell display whether 10 was greater than 5, then we could write the following if/then construct:

```
If (10 -gt  5)
{
    Write-Host "Yes"
}
```

Remember gt is the PowerShell switch for greater than, which we learned in Chapter 6. We used Write-Host in the previous example in this chapter as well.

If we run this at a PowerShell prompt, we get what is shown in Figure 7.4.

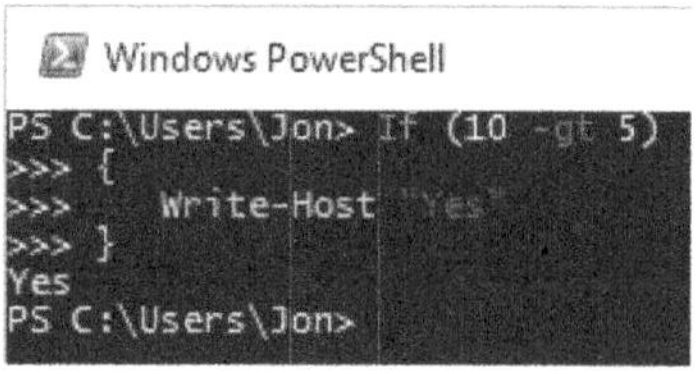

Figure 7.4: A simple if/then test.

That's kind of simple and probably not going to be a ton of use in your administrative duties. To make the construct a little more functional, you can add more
nests to the if/then block. Again, these execute in a progression; in programming
parlance, this is known as a serial construct, meaning one comparison has to finish, then the next one, and as soon as one finishes, the comparisons stop. It
would look like this:

```
If (10 -gt   11)
{
    Write-Host "Yes"
} elseif (11 -gt 10)
{
    Write-Host "This time, yes"
}
```

You should be able to follow that one pretty easily. Here is the result, as shown
in Figure 7.5.

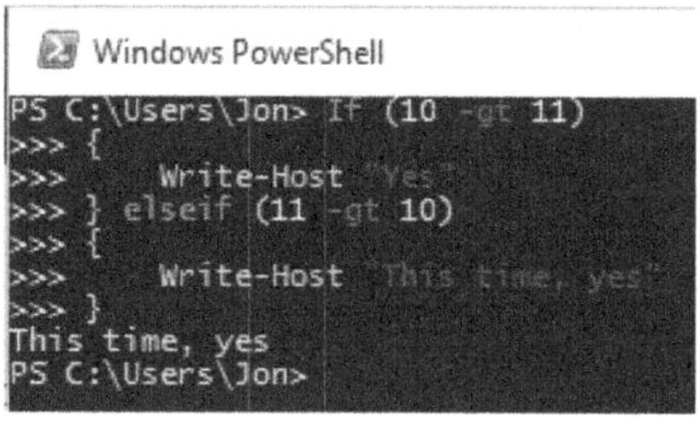

Figure 7.5: A more complicated if/then test.

Let's look in detail at what is happening there. The first logical comparison (is 10
greater than 11? No) is false, so PowerShell moves on to the next one (is 11 greater

than 10? Yes), and prints the `Write-Host` line I wrote for that test. In constructs like these, when you're testing, it's best to have different output for each test. If I had chosen Yes for both constructs, and then run the script, I would not have been able to tell which comparison test was producing the Yes. There's no differentiation. Here, I added "This time" so I could tell what was actually happening in the script.

You can include a bunch of these `elseif` blocks in your script; theoretically there is no maximum. It's a great way to establish conditions before you do something. For instance, if I only wanted to move mailboxes where the user's region was in the United States, then I could use an If statement to get at the mailbox properties and then write the code for the move within the curly braces. Or maybe I have a machine with a pesky startup problem because of an interaction with an old piece of software. So, I need to write a script that I set off as a scheduled task that checks a service after a minute or two and, if it is stopped (there's my comparison), starts the service (there's my code). Hopefully you can see the applications of this type of PowerShell construct.

Finally, you can choose to include an else block in your if/then construct, which runs as the alternative ending for your script if all the ifs and elseifs do not actually evaluate and run their code. Then the else block can do something to conclude the script. The else block is written at the very end and *does not* include a parenthetical comparison statement; you leave it off.

Here's an example: I might make a series of comparisons like this, and then make a statement of exasperation at the end:

```
If (10 -gt  11)
{
    Write-Host "Yes"
} elseif (11 -lt 10)
{
    Write-Host "This time, yes"
} elseif (20 -gt 40)
{
    Write-Host "Third time was a charm"
} else {
    Write-Host "You're really terrible at math, aren't
you?"
}
```

If I run this in PowerShell, this is what I get back from the console; take a gander at Figure 7.6.

```
PS C:\Users\Jonathan> If (10 -gt  11)
>> {
>> Write-Host "Yes"
>> } elseif (11 -lt 10)
>> {
>> Write-Host "This time, yes"
>> } elseif (20 -gt 40)
>> {
>> Write-Host "Third time was a charm"
>> } else {
>> Write-Host "You're really terrible at math, aren't you?"
>> }
>>
You're really terrible at math, aren't you?
PS C:\Users\Jonathan>
```

Figure 7.6: An even deeper if/then test.

That's if/then constructs in a nutshell.

Do While Constructs

Do While is the simplest of the looping constructs in PowerShell. What the heck does that mean? A looping construct is basically a piece of code that does the same action over and over to a set of things. In other words, it loops through a set of things, doing something to each of them, until some condition changes or that set of things is exhausted. There are two main types of looping constructs in PowerShell: a Do While loop, and another one I will explain to you in the next section.

Do While is simply a construct that says to PowerShell, do this to this set of things until some condition I tell you becomes true. It's as simple as that.

There are two ways to set up this construct. If you want a set of commands to execute at least once, and then as many times as are necessary to satisfy the condition you set up, you can simply put Do and a left curly brace on one line, the commands to execute starting on a new line after the left curly brace, and then on a new line, the right curly brace followed by While and then, within parenthesis, your conditional statement. The conditional statement again must be true or false.

For example, let's set up a variable called numbers and give it an initial value of one:

```
$numbers = 1
```

Then, let's set up a simple Do While construct that adds 1 to whatever number is already in that variable, until the variable has the number 10 in it.

```
Do {
    $numbers = $numbers + 1
                Write-Host "The current value of the
variable is $numbers"
} While ($numbers -lt 10)
```

Here's what that looks like in the console, as you can see in Figure 7.7.

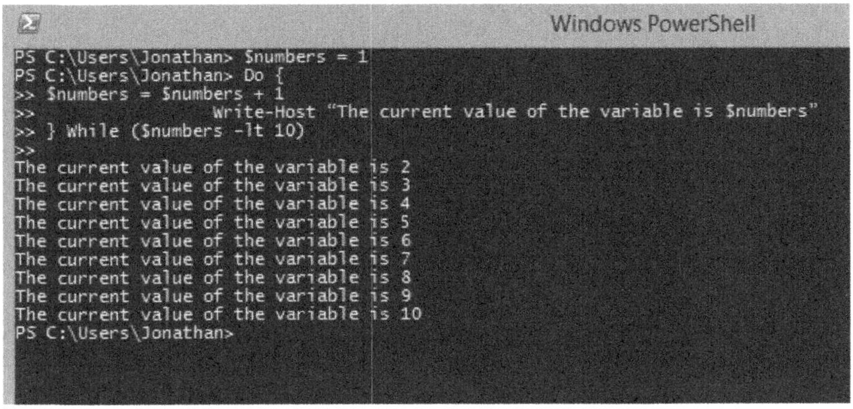

Figure 7.7: An example of a Do While construct.

You can also set up a Do While construct so that your set of commands only executes when the condition is true. You just need to eliminate the Do statement, and only use `While`.

```
While ($numbers -lt 10) {
    $numbers = $numbers + 1
                Write-Host "The current value of the
variable is $numbers"
}
```

Figure 7.8 shows what that ends up looking like.

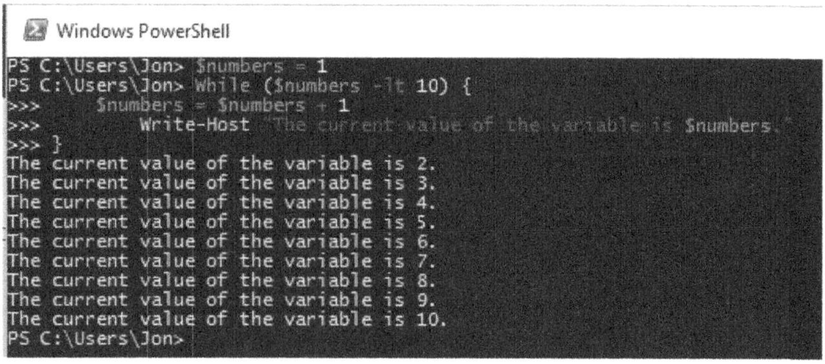

Figure 7.8: A Do While statement using just a While condition.

See if you can think of why you might use Do While statements vs. just a While loop. Bonus points (I guess these are karma points?) for writing the code for each of the scenarios.

The ForEach Construct

ForEach is the other looping construct I indicated I would tell you about. ForEach simply looks at a set of things and pulls out one at a time to look at them and, if you say so, perform some type of action or set of commands on it.

Here's how to think of this. Let's say you had a list of users sent over from your human resources department, a list of employees who had resigned in the previous quarter. You need to disable their Active Directory accounts. You can use a ForEach loop to work on this. You would say, Dear PowerShell

Here's my list of users

ForEach (user in that list)

{ disable their log on ability in Active Directory }

Note the familiar curly braces and their placement. (In developer parlance, what I just showed you in this example is called pseudocode. It's a way to break down how you would write code without taking the time to figure out the correct syntax, just as a way of making sure you have a good game plan when you approach a problem for which you need to write code to solve.) One different part of a ForEach loop is the keyword `in` that lives within that parenthetical statement. That tells PowerShell to create a single variable to hold the values that come out, one at a time, of your bigger set of things.

Let's look at a real code example using a simple set of names in a variable.

```
$names = Amy,Bob,Candice,Dick,Eunice,Frank
```

When we make a list within a variable, we have created what is known as an array, simply a matrix of sorts that PowerShell holds in memory that lets it store a bunch of things at one time.

Let's also initialize a count variable so we get a sense of how the loop is going.

```
$count = 0
```

Then, let's use a ForEach loop to count how many names we have. Remember our keyword `in`. We have to create a new variable that we can call anything we want, although we need to make sure it's a clear name so we know what we were referring to when we might have to come back to the script after a long time away. This variable holds each single name that comes out of that list we have stored in the variable `$names`. I have called this new variable `$singlename` just to make it clear it is a new variable that just holds a single value that comes out of a list. PowerShell works on that single value and then moves on, grabbing another value from the bigger list, storing it in the new single variable, acting on it based on whatever commands you have put into the loop, and then lathering, rinsing, and repeating.

```
ForEach ($singlename in $names) {
    $count += 1
            Write-Host "$singlename"
}
```

The += shorthand basically just says increment the number by whatever interval I put next, in this case 1. I then added a `Write-Host` line with the `$single-name` variable so we can get a glimpse into what value PowerShell is working on in the loop.

Finally, I'll add a simple `Write-Host` line after the end (after the right curly brace, that is) to display the count, so we can answer our question:

```
Write-Host "The total number of names is $count."
```

Figure 7.9 shows what it looks like all put together and run in PowerShell.

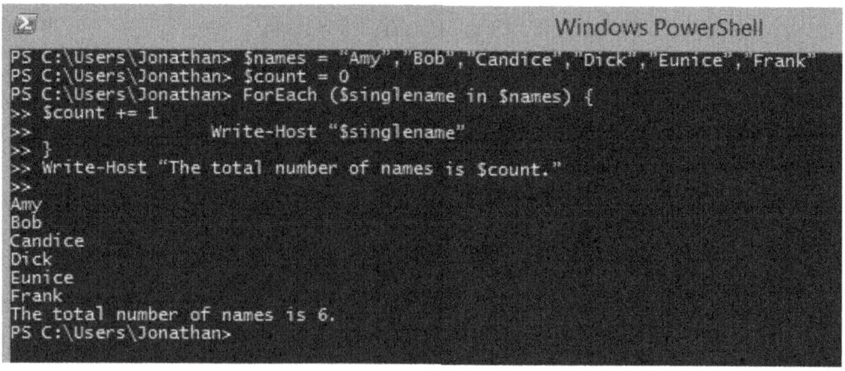

```
PS C:\Users\Jonathan> $names = "Amy","Bob","Candice","Dick","Eunice","Frank"
PS C:\Users\Jonathan> $count = 0
PS C:\Users\Jonathan> ForEach ($singlename in $names) {
>> $count += 1
>>                 Write-Host "$singlename"
>> }
>> Write-Host "The total number of names is $count."
>>
Amy
Bob
Candice
Dick
Eunice
Frank
The total number of names is 6.
PS C:\Users\Jonathan>
```

Figure 7.9: ForEach their own. Ha ha ha.

That's a ForEach loop.

Putting It All Together: Scripts to Accomplish Something Useful

I want to tie everything you learned in this chapter together with a PowerShell-based solution to a very pragmatic issue. I recently had to tackle a problem: I needed to migrate mailboxes from a virtualized Exchange 2007 server to a virtualized Exchange 2010 server running Service Pack 3. One other restriction: I could not spend any money to do it. (What can I say, the client was cheap. Also, in a related story, the client was me.)

To follow along with this section, you will need administrative access to an Exchange Server 2010 machine. But even if you don't, you can still follow along with the logic. Everything I do in this section achieves a real solution to a real problem using only the concepts we have learned thus far in the book. I happen to believe it is a really powerful demonstration of how much you have learned from this book so far.

Luckily, Exchange 2010, beginning with Service Pack 1, debuted the mailbox import and export request cmdlets as part of its PowerShell module. Harnessing those made cheap work of the import process, and I wanted to share this. First off, I exported all the mailboxes via Outlook to PST files, so that I had a folder full of PST files, all named `alias.pst`, where `alias` was the user's logon name. That made it easy to track who was who and which PST belonged to whom.

Now that I had a folder full of PSTs (which, unlike what you might expect, is nothing like Mitt Romney's "binders full of women"), I needed to get Exchange

2010 to ingest them. There are a couple of ways to perform an import over multiple mailboxes. For each of these methods, you will of course need to know the names of the PST files serving as your archives you want to import. If the PST files match the names of the mailboxes on the system to which you are importing, then you can simply use Method 1. If the names of the PST files and the mailboxes on the target system for import differ, then you will need to use the second method. (Note I don't pretend that there are no other ways to do this; this is how I did it and I found it worked well and at no cost other than my time.)

For both methods, you of course need the PSTs stored on a *network path* accessible from your target Exchange server, with read and write permissions for the EXCHANGE TRUSTED SUBSYSTEM account on that file path. I'm assuming you already know how to set NTFS permissions, so I won't bother with that here.

You will also need to grant your user account the mailbox import-export role; you may need to close and reopen your Exchange Management Shell window if you adjust the permissions while you have a current session of your own open. Here's the quick Exchange Management Shell PowerShell command to grant these rights:

```
New-ManagementRoleAssignment -Role "Mailbox Import Export" youraccountname
```

Be sure to replace `youraccountname` with your alias.

Method 1

Method 1 is very simple for each construct that first grabs a list of all mailboxes you have created in your target Exchange environment. Then, for each of those mailboxes, the script grabs an identically named PST file from a certain network path and creates a mailbox import request for them. This is a super simple way to perform a mass import, but you need to make sure your names match exactly, or an error will be thrown for the mismatched user.

```
foreach ($mailbox in (Get-Mailbox))
{
    New-MailboxImportRequest -Mailbox $mailbox -
FilePath "\\server\pstimportfolder\$($mail-
box.Alias).pst"
}
```

Method 2

This method uses a comma separated value (CSV) file that has just two values in it for each line: user, for the username, and pstfile, for the filename (without the preceding folder names) that maps to each specified user. Since you can specify the name of the PST file, the names on the files and the target mailboxes do not have to match, which makes this the more versatile method, although it makes the script a little bit complex.

Here is an example of the CSV file:

```
user,pstfile
jhassell,jhassell.pst
finance,finance.pst
```

And here's the script.

```
$pstdata = Import-CSV C:\pick-your-path\pstimport.csv

ForEach ($pst in $pstdata)
{

    $user = $pst.user
    $pstfile = $pst.pstfile
    $pstpath = "\\server1\pst\$pstfile"

    Get-ChildItem -Recurse -path $pstpath -Filter
*.pst | Foreach-Object {
        New-MailboxImportRequest -FilePath $_.FullName
-Mailbox $user -Name "Import $user $($_.Name)" -
BadItemLimit 15 -ConflictResolutionOption KeepAll -
Confirm:$false
        }
}
```

Don't forget to change the path in the $pstpath variable to the actual server and share names for where your PST files are stored. Also, do not neglect to change the path to your CSV file the script uses to assign PST files to their respective mailboxes.

Two other things to think about here:

- As you might expect, you can also stick a -whatif flag after the final part of the `new-mailboximportrequest` to make sure you don't kick off an import process you do not want or to check your work.
- You can also use this to import archive mailboxes in Exchange 2010. Just add the `IsArchive` flag to the `New-Mailboximportrequest` part of the script, too.

A Simple Backup Strategy for Smaller Exchange Environments

All of this PST importing and exporting got me to thinking: for smaller environments or a quick-and-dirty backup, you can use PowerShell to automatically export the contents of your mailboxes to a PST.

Again, as you might expect from me at this point, a simple script will do this for you:

```
foreach ($mailbox in (Get-Mailbox))
{
    New-MailboxExportRequest -Mailbox $mailbox -
FilePath "\\server\pstexportfolder\$($mail-
box.Alias).pst"
}
```

This is obviously no substitute for a proper backup strategy or a true backup and restore product, but it's a good additional layer of protection.

You can also easily adapt the script as well by applying some scoping to the Get-Mailbox command. In this script, only the finalized results of the Get-Mailbox cmdlet will be piped to the export-request mechanism, so you can do the filtering with Get-Mailbox using, say, a where clause and export only a subset of mailboxes.

Clearing the Requests

Once your import is complete, you can clear out the import requests with this entry to keep your system nice and tidy:

```
Get-MailboxImportRequest | where {$_.status -eq "Com-
pleted"} | Remove-MailboxImportRequest
```

At the risk of being obvious, if you are doing the poor man's export and backup method I showed you above, you can clear those requests out with this slightly modified cmdlet:

```
Get-MailboxExportRequest | where {$_.status -eq "Com-
pleted"} | Remove-MailboxExportRequest
```

The Last Word

As I mentioned, my goal for this chapter, the seventh (!), of *Learning PowerShell* was to show you how to put together some simple scripts. We've covered a lot in this chapter: variables, how to make scripts, and how to add some logic to your scripting. Then I took a very real issue I encountered recently and showed you the solution to various facets of it using PowerShell scripts that touch on all the concepts we have learned in this book up until now. Congratulations! Onward!

Chapter 8
More Work with Objects

Welcome to Chapter 8 of *Learning PowerShell*!

As I mentioned at the conclusion of Chapter 7, if you've completely read, digested, and understood all the concepts and practices I have taught you—and you have put those skills to the test in your own lab with your own test system—you have graduated from a total beginner to a beginner. I assumed at the beginning of the book that you had absolutely zero experience at PowerShell, were not a developer, and that I had to essentially spoon-feed you the information to help you achieve competence. But now you know how to find PowerShell commands, how to run them, how to pipe them together, how to sort them, how to filter them, how to create simple scripts, how to loop over certain commands in various forms and increments, and you've done several practical labs that put together all these concepts, all tied up nicely and neatly in a bow.

Now's the start of the slightly more advanced *but still very much beginner* level material in this book. I don't want you to remain a total beginner by the time you finish this book. Rather, I want you to feel confident that while you don't know everything about PowerShell, you know enough to be dangerous (read, productive) and that you know enough to find out how to carry out some task you might not immediately know how to carry out beforehand.

The core place to begin with this slightly more in-depth material is objects. You received a good introduction to objects in a previous chapter, but since objects are everything in PowerShell's output, you can do some cool stuff without a ton more work, mainly because PowerShell does the heavy lifting. You just have to massage the syntax.

Let's take a look and you'll see what I mean.

Comparing Two Objects

One of the key tools in any scripter's arsenal is the ability to compare two different things against each other and figure out the differences. For example, wouldn't it be useful if you could:

— compare security event log entries around the time of an attack, using a log from a compromised system and an uncompromised system to see if there are any clues about how your security was broken

DOI 10.1515/9781501506673-008

- compare a list of server roles installed on a machine to one that should be installed on all machines of a specific type (for example, a mail server template), and point out which roles might be missing so that they can be added
- compare a list of mailboxes you have with a list of mailboxes that you need to put on legal hold and then identify which ones might not have had the legal hold enabled, or find dates when the legal hold was enabled, or …

You get the picture. We talked about filtering and limiting to get at a subset of objects to which we wanted to do something using a PowerShell command. Usually, you need to do something to only some of the things, and filtering and limiting using `Where-Object` and the like are a good way to do that. But sometimes the set of things you want to do something *to* needs to come from a list of differences between two things, and that's a powerful way to get at a set of things on which to run operations, too.

I bet you're thinking, "Hmm, I wonder if there's a command for that." And you'd be right. I am sure by now you could figure out how to find that command to *compare* two different *objects*. But in the interests of getting on with it, I'll just tell you now that that the command is called, conveniently, `Compare-Object`. Let's take a look at how it works.

Looking at `Compare-Object`

The command `Compare-Object` at its core compares two objects: a reference object and a difference object. The reference object is like the template, and it is the object that the command will use to point out what's different than that object in the difference object.

Think of the reference object as A and the difference object as B. `Compare-Object` will tell you how B is different from A. The syntax says you need to put the reference object first and then the difference object. How do we know this? Because when we run `Get-Help Compare-Object` we see the following:

```
Syntax
     Compare-Object [-referenceObject] PSObject[] [-
differenceObject] PSObject[]
          [-syncWindow int] [-property Object[]] [-
caseSensitive]
            [-culture string] [-excludeDifferent] [-
includeEqual]
```

```
      [-passThru] [CommonParameters]

Key
   -referenceObject PSObject[]
      Object(s) used as a reference for comparison.

   -differenceObject PSObject[]
      Object(s) to compare to the reference ob-
ject(s).

   -syncWindow int
      The search region where an attempt is made to
re-sync the order if there is no match.
      The Default=[Int32]::MaxValue
      (In PowerShell 1.0 this default was just 5
which is often too low)

   -property Object[]
      Properties of the objects to compare.

   -caseSensitive
      Make comparisons case-sensitive.

   -culture string
      The culture to use for comparisons.

   -excludeDifferent
      Display only the characteristics of compared
objects that are equal.

   -includeEqual
      Displays characteristics of compared objects
that are equal.
      By default only differences are displayed.

   -passThru
      Pass the object created by this cmdlet through
the pipeline.
```

```
CommonParameters:
     -Verbose, -Debug, -ErrorAction, -ErrorVariable,
-WarningAction, -WarningVariable,
     -OutBuffer -OutVariable.
```

You can see `-referenceObject` and `-differenceObject` are positional parameters because only the parameter name is enclosed in brackets. I suppose you could name the parameters if you wanted to, in which case (again as you know) you can include the parameters in any order, but I recommend just learning that the syntax of the command is something like "here's my template, and then tell me how this is different than my template."

Let's take a simple example: say we have two simple plain text files. Here's one.

```
Made on Monday
Hello everyone!
This is the first text file.
```

Here's the other.

```
Made on Tuesday
Hello everyone!
This is the first text file.
```

We can create those text files in Notepad or any other text editor. Save the first text file as `1.txt` and save the other as `2.txt`.

Next, we need to read those files into memory. Why? Because we need to turn them into objects so that `Compare-Object` can work. It doesn't work with text files per se, but it can work with the string objects that reading in a text file into a PowerShell command can produce. What command can we use to *get* some *content* out of a text file and into memory? Ah, yes, the `Get-Content` feature. But how do we store objects in a holding place in memory? By creating a variable; right! And recall that we can put the output of commands into a variable simply by declaring the variable and then typing out the command, like so:

```
$1 = Get-Content 1.txt
$2 = Get-Content 2.txt
```

So then we can do our `Compare-Object` fun. Let's roll with it. We'll say that the first file, `1.txt`, is our reference object so we'll use the `$1` variable to represent that in the command. We will further say that the second file, `2.txt`, is our difference object, so we'll use the `$2` variable to represent that in the command. All we need to do now is type the command into our PowerShell console window.

```
Compare-Object $1 $2
```

Figure 8.1 what I get when I run the above sequence on my system.

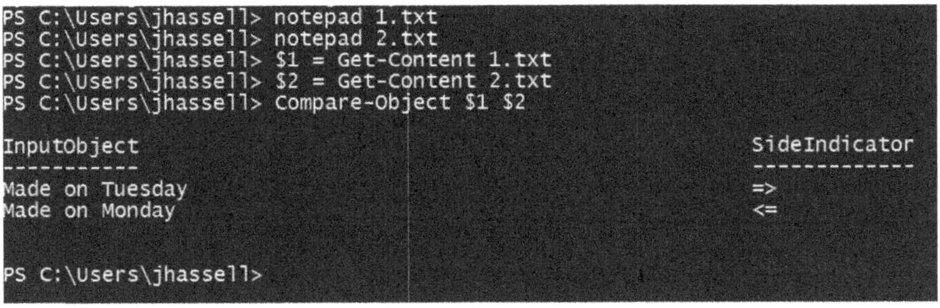

```
PS C:\Users\jhassell> notepad 1.txt
PS C:\Users\jhassell> notepad 2.txt
PS C:\Users\jhassell> $1 = Get-Content 1.txt
PS C:\Users\jhassell> $2 = Get-Content 2.txt
PS C:\Users\jhassell> Compare-Object $1 $2

InputObject                                          SideIndicator
-----------                                          -------------
Made on Tuesday                                      =>
Made on Monday                                       <=


PS C:\Users\jhassell>
```

Figure 8.1: Running the `Compare-Object` command for the first time.

The result is pretty interesting and intuitive, but let me go over it to avoid doubt. You see something like:

=>

and

<=

These indicators are called *side indicators*, and they show in which direction a property that ends up being *different* in each file goes. In this example, you could see that the object "Made on Tuesday" has a => for its side indicator, which should tell you "Made on Tuesday" appears in the difference object version of the file. Further, "Made on Monday" has a <= for its side indicator, which should tell you that "Made on Monday" appears in the reference object version of the file.

You don't see any of the other objects in the file (each object is basically one separate line in the text file, so "Made on [day]" was an object, "Hello everyone!" was an object, and "This is the first text file" was also an object) because the other two objects were the same in each file. There were no differences, so `Compare-Object` simply leaves them out.

TIP: **You might find examples of Compare-Object on the Internet, except you might not know** it at first because you'll see a bunch of people using its alias, `diff`. `diff` is a Unix command and many folks who use command line interfaces like PowerShell come from Unix backgrounds. So a lot of PowerShell commands that manipulate objects and text strings have aliases named after their Unix counterparts. I won't be using these aliases in this book because I think it can be confusing for beginners and other learners, but the nomenclature is something to be aware of as you start looking into using `Compare-Object` in various scenarios in the wild and you Google or Bing for others' examples.

Another Example

For the next example, I'll borrow from the PowerShell.com blog, an excellent place to go for reference and script ideas as you grow in your mastery of PowerShell. I got the idea for this tip from the following URL: http://powershell.com/cs/blogs/tips/archive/2010/12/31/comparing-services.aspx.

Let's say you have a couple of systems and one of them is behaving strangely. You cannot quite figure out the culprit, but maybe there is a problem with a service being stopped that ought to be started or which is configured for startup incorrectly. You can use PowerShell to compare the services that are running on each machine and maybe figure out what's wrong with your failing system.

First off, you need to use the healthy system as the reference object. We'll declare a variable called `$system1` and use the `Get-Service` command to get a list of services from that system.

```
$system1 = Get-Service -ComputerName HEALTHYSYSTEM
```

Then, we'll declare another variable called `$system2` and use the `Get-Service` command identically to store a list of services from that system.

```
$system2 = Get-Service -ComputerName FAILINGSYSTEM
```

Then, we can use the `Compare-Object` command.

```
Compare-Object -ReferenceObject $system1 -DifferenceObject $system2
```

But maybe we want to get a little fancier and display only the properties we care about. We could do that using the `-Property` parameter and selecting only the properties for display that might tell us something interesting. You already know how to find out what the properties of an object are (hint: pipe `Get-Service` to `Get-Member`).

```
Compare-Object -ReferenceObject $system1 -Difference-
Object $system2 -Property Name,Status
```

Super. But now let's sort by the name of the service so we have a nice alphabetical list for easy browsing and troubleshooting.

```
Compare-Object -ReferenceObject $system1 -Difference-
Object $system2 -Property Name,Status -passThru |
Sort-Object Name
```

Perfect.

Selecting Objects

Until now we've been working with the whole shebang: piping a bunch of objects to another command, doing a little work, piping that same bunch of objects to another command, and then lathering, rinsing, and repeating. But there's a way to limit and filter the objects you work with at each step, which makes for better scripting. In other words, there is a way to *select* an *object*.

Another tool in your arsenal is the ability to select only the objects you care about from a collection (remember a collection is a group of objects, properties, methods, and events). Rather than try to sort through all the objects any given command returns, there exists `Select-Object`, which lets you pick and choose from that gamut of options and process only the objects you care about. Let's look at this in more detail and see how it works.

Selecting a Certain Number of Objects

You can choose to select the first few or last few objects that a command produces. You'll probably find the option to find the last few objects is far more useful in practice than the option to select the first few, but both abilities are there. For example, you can say `Select-Object -First n` where n is the number of objects you'd like to see. You can also say `Select-Object -Last` n to do the same for the last objects instead of the first in line.

You'll probably want to use `Select-Object` in conjunction with sorting objects by a certain property in ascending or descending order. Recall from an earlier chapter that to *sort* an *object*, we would use the `Sort-Object` command.

For instance, I might want to look at the last five files written to a certain directory on my system. In that case, I'd want to get the files, sort them by last write time, and then use `Select-Object` to find the last five files. You do all of this with—you guessed it—the pipeline.

```
Get-ChildItem c:\files | Sort-Object -Property Last-
WriteTime | Select-Object -Last 5
```

Or here is another practical application: a user's home directory is filling up and he is bumping up against his quota. You have a busy day and you need a quick win to get this user under quota so you both can get back to your task lists. So you just want to find his biggest file and move it somewhere else and deal with it later. In this case, you would use `Get-ChildItem c:\users\ username\documents` to do the directory listing, then pipe that over to `Sort-Object` to sort by length in a descending order so that the largest items pop up to the top, and then use `Select-Object` to find the biggest two files that ought to be moved to free up space. That all could be accomplished in the following one (!) command:

```
Get-ChildItem c:\users\username\documents | Sort-Object
-Property Length -Descending | Select-Object -First 2
```

Selecting Certain Properties

You can also use `Select-Object` to select individual or multiple properties of any given object among the many usually available. Do you remember how to find out the properties that are available for any given object? Yes, that's done with `Get-Member`.

For instance, let's look at our old standby command, `Get-EventLog -LogName Application -Newest 5`. Pipe that to `Get-Member` and let's see what we end up with.

```
Get-EventLog -LogName Application -Newest 5 | Get-Member
```

We'll see a few options, a sample of which is provided in Figure 8.2.

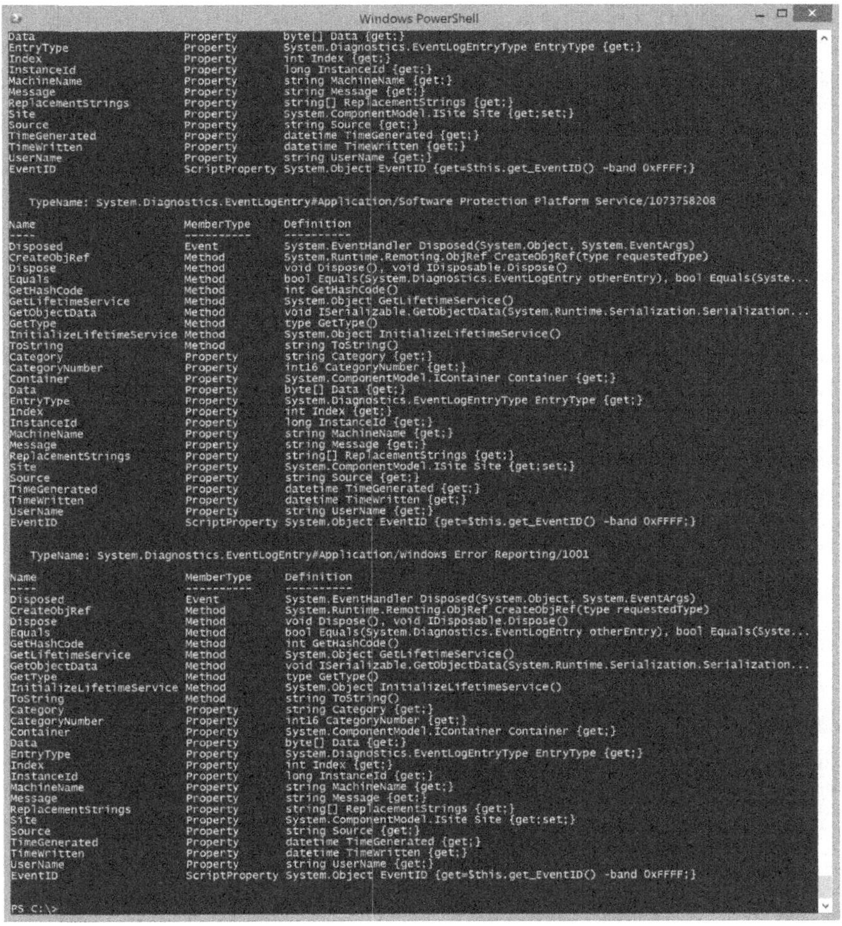

```
Windows PowerShell
Data                       Property       byte[] Data {get;}
EntryType                  Property       System.Diagnostics.EventLogEntryType EntryType {get;}
Index                      Property       int Index {get;}
InstanceId                 Property       long InstanceId {get;}
MachineName                Property       string MachineName {get;}
Message                    Property       string Message {get;}
ReplacementStrings         Property       string[] ReplacementStrings {get;}
Site                       Property       System.ComponentModel.ISite Site {get;set;}
Source                     Property       string Source {get;}
TimeGenerated              Property       datetime TimeGenerated {get;}
TimeWritten                Property       datetime TimeWritten {get;}
UserName                   Property       string UserName {get;}
EventID                    ScriptProperty System.Object EventID {get=$this.get_EventID() -band 0xFFFF;}


   TypeName: System.Diagnostics.EventLogEntry#Application/Software Protection Platform Service/1073758208

Name                       MemberType     Definition
----                       ----------     ----------
Disposed                   Event          System.EventHandler Disposed(System.Object, System.EventArgs)
CreateObjRef               Method         System.Runtime.Remoting.ObjRef CreateObjRef(type requestedType)
Dispose                    Method         void Dispose(), void IDisposable.Dispose()
Equals                     Method         bool Equals(System.Diagnostics.EventLogEntry otherEntry), bool Equals(Syste...
GetHashCode                Method         int GetHashCode()
GetLifetimeService         Method         System.Object GetLifetimeService()
GetObjectData              Method         void ISerializable.GetObjectData(System.Runtime.Serialization.Serialization...
GetType                    Method         type GetType()
InitializeLifetimeService  Method         System.Object InitializeLifetimeService()
ToString                   Method         string ToString()
Category                   Property       string Category {get;}
CategoryNumber             Property       int16 CategoryNumber {get;}
Container                  Property       System.ComponentModel.IContainer Container {get;}
Data                       Property       byte[] Data {get;}
EntryType                  Property       System.Diagnostics.EventLogEntryType EntryType {get;}
Index                      Property       int Index {get;}
InstanceId                 Property       long InstanceId {get;}
MachineName                Property       string MachineName {get;}
Message                    Property       string Message {get;}
ReplacementStrings         Property       string[] ReplacementStrings {get;}
Site                       Property       System.ComponentModel.ISite Site {get;set;}
Source                     Property       string Source {get;}
TimeGenerated              Property       datetime TimeGenerated {get;}
TimeWritten                Property       datetime TimeWritten {get;}
UserName                   Property       string UserName {get;}
EventID                    ScriptProperty System.Object EventID {get=$this.get_EventID() -band 0xFFFF;}


   TypeName: System.Diagnostics.EventLogEntry#Application/Windows Error Reporting/1001

Name                       MemberType     Definition
----                       ----------     ----------
Disposed                   Event          System.EventHandler Disposed(System.Object, System.EventArgs)
CreateObjRef               Method         System.Runtime.Remoting.ObjRef CreateObjRef(type requestedType)
Dispose                    Method         void Dispose(), void IDisposable.Dispose()
Equals                     Method         bool Equals(System.Diagnostics.EventLogEntry otherEntry), bool Equals(Syste...
GetHashCode                Method         int GetHashCode()
GetLifetimeService         Method         System.Object GetLifetimeService()
GetObjectData              Method         void ISerializable.GetObjectData(System.Runtime.Serialization.Serialization...
GetType                    Method         type GetType()
InitializeLifetimeService  Method         System.Object InitializeLifetimeService()
ToString                   Method         string ToString()
Category                   Property       string Category {get;}
CategoryNumber             Property       int16 CategoryNumber {get;}
Container                  Property       System.ComponentModel.IContainer Container {get;}
Data                       Property       byte[] Data {get;}
EntryType                  Property       System.Diagnostics.EventLogEntryType EntryType {get;}
Index                      Property       int Index {get;}
InstanceId                 Property       long InstanceId {get;}
MachineName                Property       string MachineName {get;}
Message                    Property       string Message {get;}
ReplacementStrings         Property       string[] ReplacementStrings {get;}
Site                       Property       System.ComponentModel.ISite Site {get;set;}
Source                     Property       string Source {get;}
TimeGenerated              Property       datetime TimeGenerated {get;}
TimeWritten                Property       datetime TimeWritten {get;}
UserName                   Property       string UserName {get;}
EventID                    ScriptProperty System.Object EventID {get=$this.get_EventID() -band 0xFFFF;}

PS C:\>
```

Figure 8.2: Finding available properties we can use in conjunction with `Select-Object`.

Among others, we can see `EventID` and `TimeGenerated` are interesting properties, so let's pipe that command to `Select-Object` and use its `-Property` parameter to select only those two properties for our resulting display.

```
Get-EventLog -LogName Application -Newest 5 | Select-
Object -Property EventID,TimeGenerated
```

Figure 8.3 shows what we get as a result.

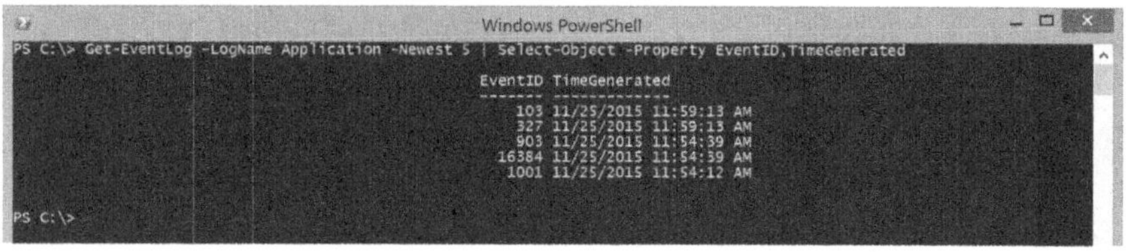

Figure 8.3: The use of `Select-Object` within properties.

That's great, but why is it formatted so ugly? Why is the table sort of off center on my screen? There's a longer, more technical explanation, but at this point, suffice it to say that PowerShell isn't sure how to format this and so it takes a guess. Sometimes that guess is as wildly off as my wife thinks my eye for color is: read, horribly off. One trick if you get this sort of funky weird formatting is to pipe the output of your last command to the `Format-Table` command and use the `-AutoSize` parameter, and PowerShell will build a table from scratch that looks a lot better. Figure 8.4 what we get if we use this trick.

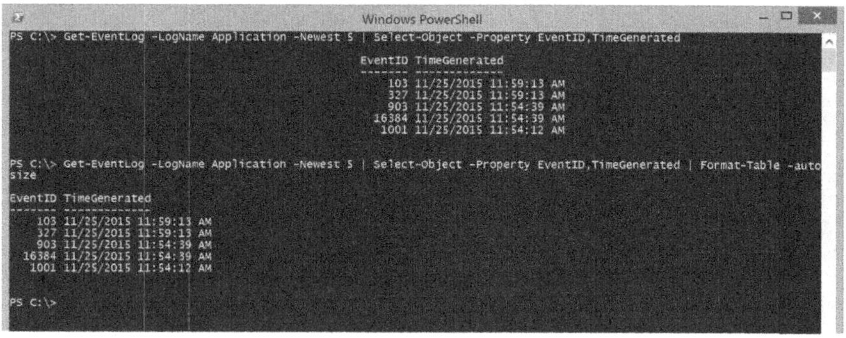

Figure 8.4: A nicely formatted list, courtesy of table formatting and the autosize feature.

Grouping Objects with Common Characteristics

What if you want to *group* an *object* by its common characteristics? You are in luck, my friend. However, the Group-Object command is one you need to understand, but that is a little abstract without a practical example that would enable you to see what's going on. I am going to attempt to explain it to you first, if for no other reason than to give you context about the command, but don't worry if it doesn't make sense, as I'll show you some examples where we're using Group-Object to get some things done.

Put simply, Group-Object groups objects together that have the same value. It puts objects together that share the same characteristic, making it easier to either get information or to do something to that common set of objects. For instance, every Windows system has Task Manager installed, and as part of Task Manager, you can see a list of services. Figure 8.5 shows an example.

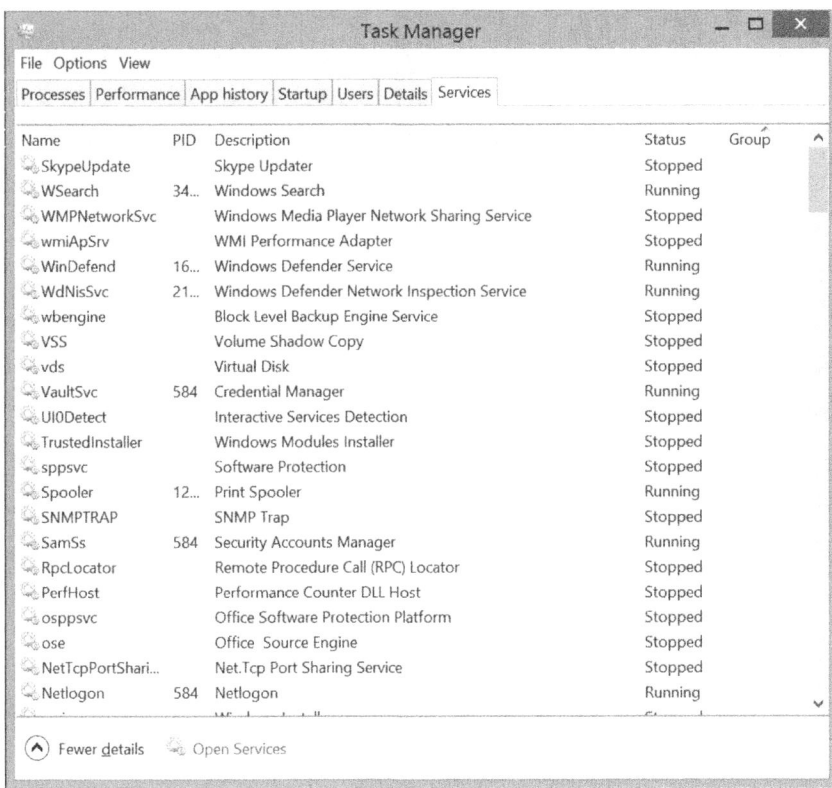

Figure 8.5: A list of services as displayed by Task Manager on a Windows 8.1 system.

With PowerShell, we can get a similar listing via the `Get-Service` command, as shown in Figure 8.6.

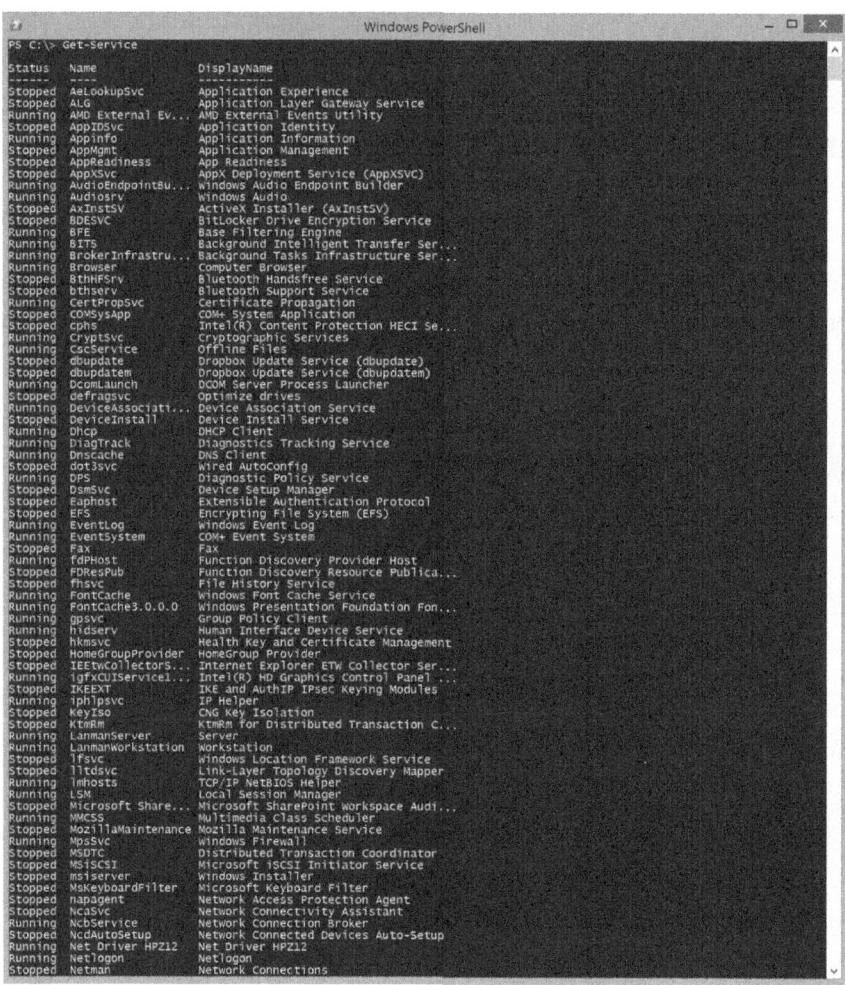

Figure 8.6: A list of services as displayed by PowerShell on a Windows 8.1 system.

But what we can do with PowerShell is group each individual service (which, as you know, is represented as an object in the pipeline after you run `Get-Service`) by a property it has. Just from the above display, you know one of the properties you can use with `Get-Service` is `Status`, so what happens if we use:

```
Get-Service | Group-Object -Property Status
```

What happens is shown in Figure 8.7.

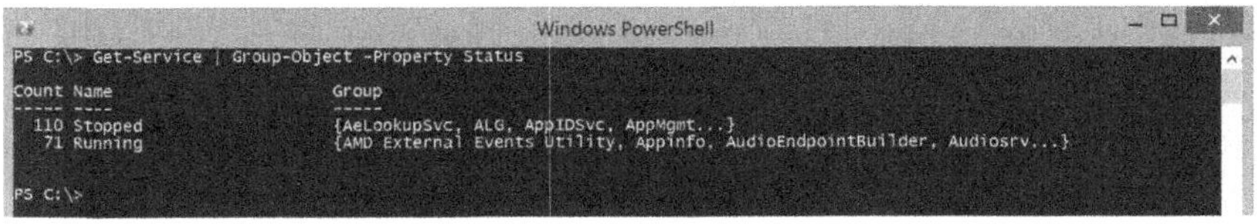

Figure 8.7: A list of services as displayed by PowerShell on a Windows 8.1 system, grouped by status.

When is this sort of thing useful? Here are a couple of useful examples.

- **Finding out which event log messages are most common.** This is good log management when you want to find out what is happening most on your system. Again, a good way to get a quick win if there is a problem: let the squeakiest wheel get the grease. This command gets the last 2,500 events from the Application event log, groups them by Event ID # (tip: look up event IDs on EventID.net), sorts them by the number of times each event ID happens (which is the count property from the object that Group-Object returns, so that's why the operation works) and then formats the output nicely to a table using the -Autosize parameter.

```
Get-EventLog -LogName Application -Newest 2500 |
Group-Object -Property eventid | Sort-Object Count -
descending | Format-Table Count, Name -autosize
```

The result is in Figure 8.8.

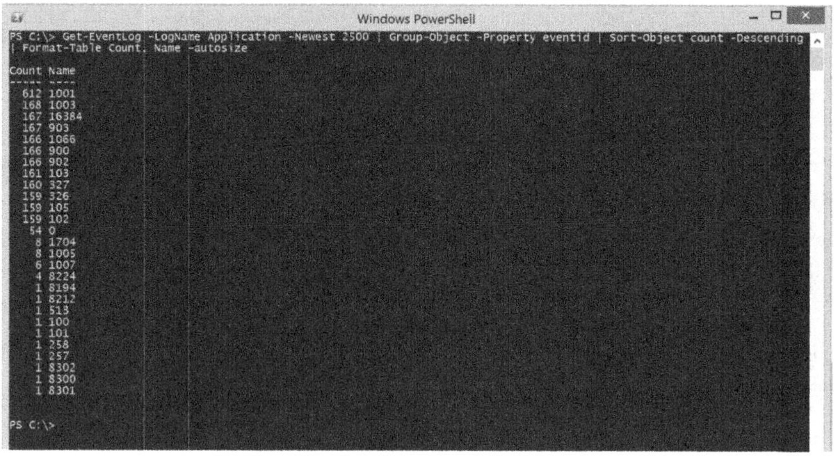

Figure 8.8: The first practical example of using `Group-Object`.

- **Finding out common error messages and how often they occur.** In a similar vein, this command will find the most common error messages and group them by event ID as well. This command gets the last 2,500 events from the Application event log, sorts them by event ID, uses a Where construct to find only events that have an error type associated with them, groups that resulting set by eventid, and then nicely formats the table.

```
Get-EventLog -LogName Application -Newest 2500 | Sort-
Object -Property eventid | Where {$_.EntryType -eq "Er-
ror"} | Group-Object -Property eventid | Format-Table -
AutoSize
```

That command's result is in Figure 8.9.

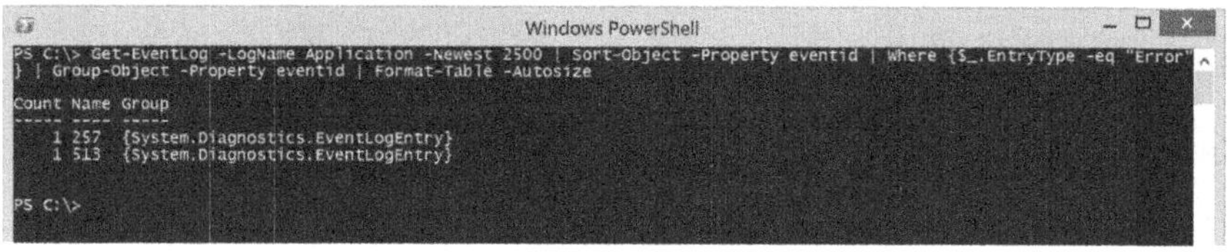

Figure 8.9: The second practical example of using `Group-Object`.

Hash Tables

Put on your advanced thinking caps for this section. I'm going to get abstract with you here, but as far as I know there is no way around it. I'm going to try to simplify this as much as possible. Still, hash tables are a *very* useful tool to have in your arsenal. It just takes a while to both (a) understand them and their use fully and (b) wrap your head around the *extremely funky* syntax that they use. Really, the syntax is unforgiveable.

Hash tables are a fancy way of saying a table full of single pieces of information many times over. Those single pieces are known as name-value pairs, or key-value pairs, as you might sometimes see them called. These pairs store a single piece of data, and the key is the descriptive word about the data and the value is the actual piece of data.

A common example of key-value pairs are a list of United States states and their capitals. We might call our key-value pair table "StateCapitals," for instance, and within that table, each state would be the key and each state's capital would be the value. We can create a sample table just to demonstrate how this would look.

```
TABLE NAME: StateCapitals

Key                 Value
---                 -----
North Carolina      Raleigh
California          Sacramento
New York            Albany
Florida             Tallahassee
Texas               Austin
```

And so on. Again, in a table for state capitals, the key would describe the state and the value would describe the capital, the thing that is in question.

Another example could be NFL teams and their mascots.

```
TABLE NAME: NFLMascots

Key                 Value
---                 -----
Carolina            Panther
New England         Patriot
Seattle             Seahawk
```

```
Dallas              Cowboy
Atlanta             Falcon
```

Again, in a table for professional football team mascots, the key would describe the team and the value would describe the actual mascot, the thing in question.

A *hash table* is actually just a table full of those key value pairs. You can start off a hash table as the value of a variable, and then you simply place an at sign (@), a left curly brace, and then use `"key1"` = `"value1"; "key2" = "value2"` and so on. Let's use both of the above "spelled-out" tables as examples.

```
$StateCapitals = @{"North Carolina" = "Raleigh"; "Cal-
ifornia" = "Sacramento"; "New York" = "Albany"; "Flor-
ida" = "Tallahassee"; "Texas" = "Austin"}
$NFLMascots = @{"Carolina" = "Panther"; "New England"
= "Patriot"; "Seattle" = "Seahawk"; "Dallas" = "Cowboy
"; "Atlanta" = "Falcon"}
```

Enter those into your PowerShell window now to get a feel for how they work. To check on them, just enter the variable's name at the prompt to display its value, which, if you typed correctly, should be the hash table. Figure 8.10 shows an example of this on my system.

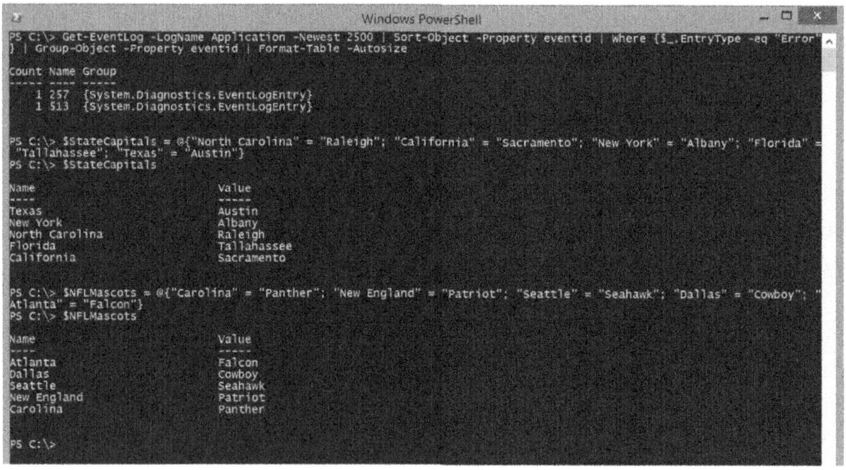

Figure 8.10: Entering two new hash tables into memory.

That's how you create a hash table at its most basic. Now why is this important? Hash tables are important because some PowerShell commands will understand hash tables as values for their parameters, and one of the most common commands you would use in this scenario is Select-Object. Specifically, when you're using Select-Object to pick properties to display, what happens if the content of those properties in the output isn't what you expected? Or what if the name of the property is one thing, but the command to which you want to pipe that output expects the same content to be called something else entirely? In that case, you would use hash tables along with Select-Object.

Select-Object accepts hash tables formatted with two specific key-value pairs. Well, more specifically, it needs two keys to be present. One key is Name, and the value of Name is used for the column header. You can use this to rewrite the names of column headers to be something else. The other key Select-Object needs is called Expression and the value of that key needs to be a script or PowerShell code. It can be a simple script or simple code, within curly braces ({ and }) but that is what Select-Object expects there.

For this book, I'll talk about but one aspect of using hash tables with Select-Object: the ability to rewrite column names. Let's take a simple example. If you run Get-Process from the PowerShell console, you get a nice table with handles, a bunch of statistics, and a column header called ProcessName. What if you want to rewrite that table so that it only shows the name of the process, but instead calls that column The Name of the Process rather than ProcessName?

You would create a hash table to do just that. That hash table is going to be built like this: first, you use Select-Object because, well, that's the command. Then you use the @ sign, which signals to PowerShell that you intend to create a hash table. Then a left curly brace { begins the contents of the table. Then, you type in the key Name—remember that has to be the name of the key when you use a hash table with Select-Object, so hard code that into your memory at this point. Then, use an =, and add the name of the column you wish to use, enclosed in quotation marks, and end with a semicolon (;). So far that looks like this:

```
Select-Object @{Name = "The Name of the Process";
```

Next up, we add the expression. It's called Expression and that's another hard coding thing to remember with hash tables used in conjunction with Select-Object. Another equals sign goes in next, followed by a left curly brace ({) to signify the beginning of a PowerShell code expression. Next, in this case, we can use the "that thing" notation ($_) that I covered in the creating scripts and loops chapter, because it represents the object in the pipeline—which in this example is the output of Get-Process. To access a property of Get-Process, we simply add a dot (.) and then the name of the property, which in this case is the original column header, ProcessName. We then add a right curly brace to signify the end of the expression, and then a final right curly brace to signal the end of the hash table itself. That has us with this final Select-Object statement.

```
Select-Object @{Name = "The Name of the Process"; Expression = {$_.ProcessName}}
```

Now just add the original Get-Process to the front of that and you'll be golden.

```
Get-Process | Select-Object @{Name = "The Name of the Process"; Expression = {$_.ProcessName}}
```

Figure 8.11 shows what that command returns.

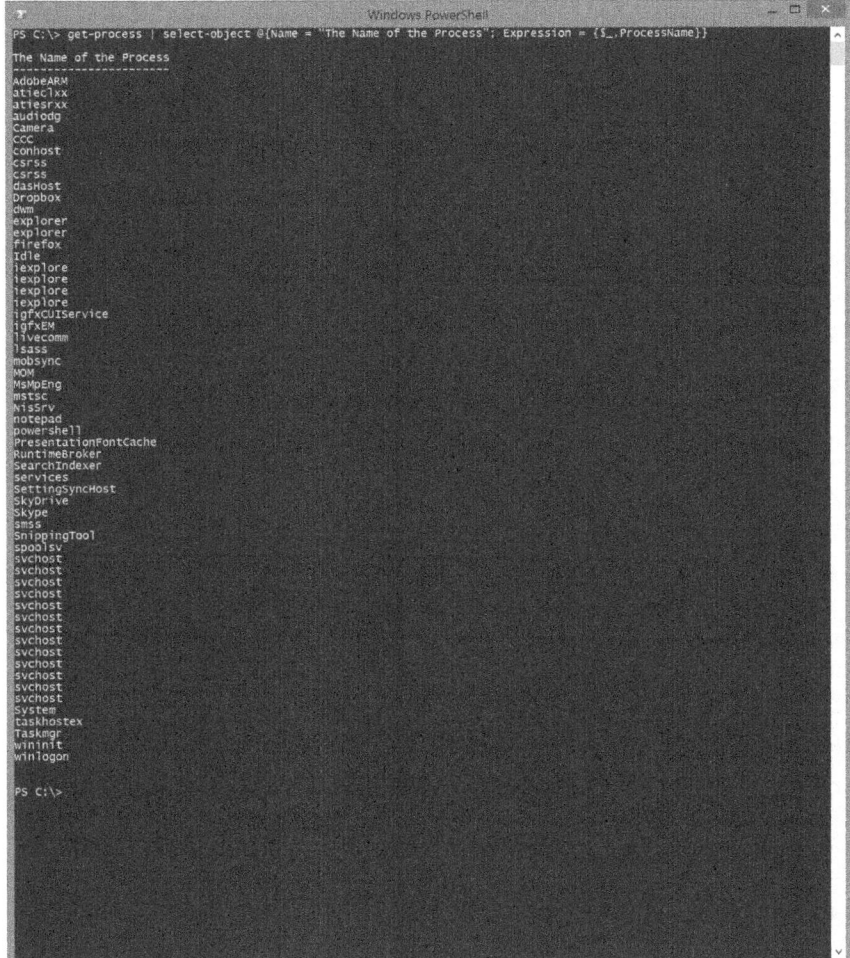

Figure 8.11: Using a hash table.

You have renamed the column totally in the pipeline, without exporting it to a file and editing the resulting file. Way to transform. You're a superhero.

You can also use multiple properties with `Select-Object`. For instance, we can just include the `Id` property with our table to get both the process ID and the transformed column. Just separate out the properties in the `Select-Object` command with commas with no spaces.

```
Get-Process | Select-Object Id,@{Name = "The Name of
the Process"; Expression = {$_.ProcessName}}
```

And that results in what you see in Figure 8.12:

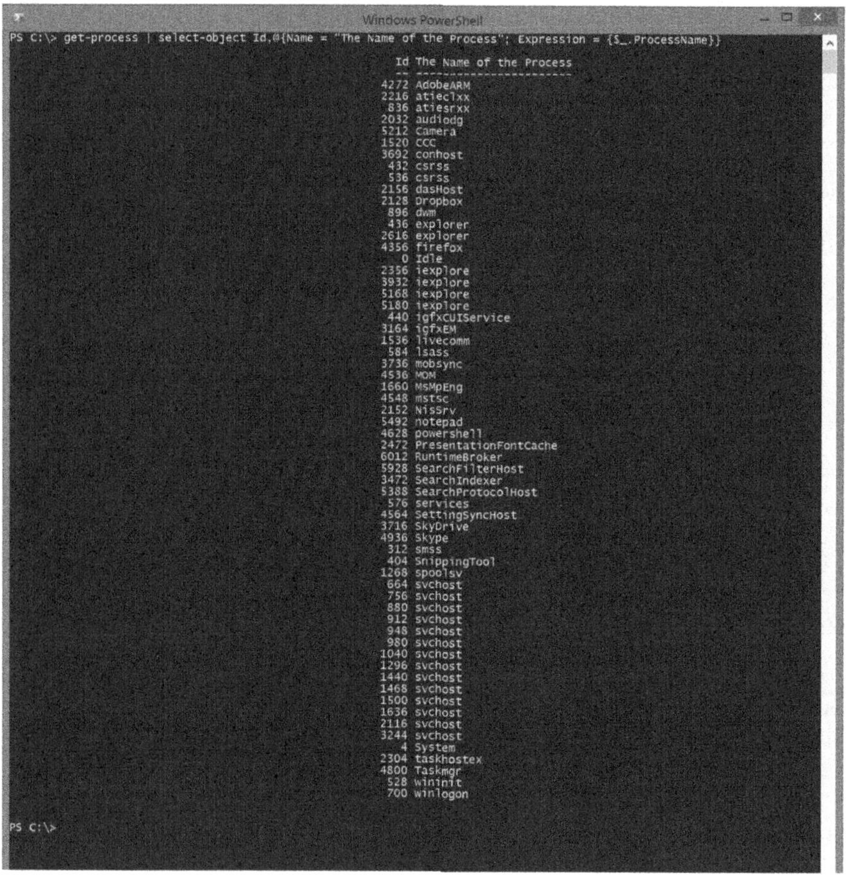

Figure 8.12: Using a hash table, redux.

And do you remember how to fix that funky off-centered formatting?

```
Get-Process | Select-Object @{Name = "The Name of the
Process"; Expression = {$_.ProcessName}} | Format-Ta-
ble -AutoSize
```

You can also use multiple hash tables. For instance, let's rewrite that ID column to call it "Process ID" and keep the other column renamed, too.

```
Get-Process | Select-Object @{Name = "Process ID"; Ex-
pression = {$_.Id}},@{Name = "The Name of the Pro-
cess"; Expression = {$_.ProcessName}} | Format-Table -
AutoSize
```

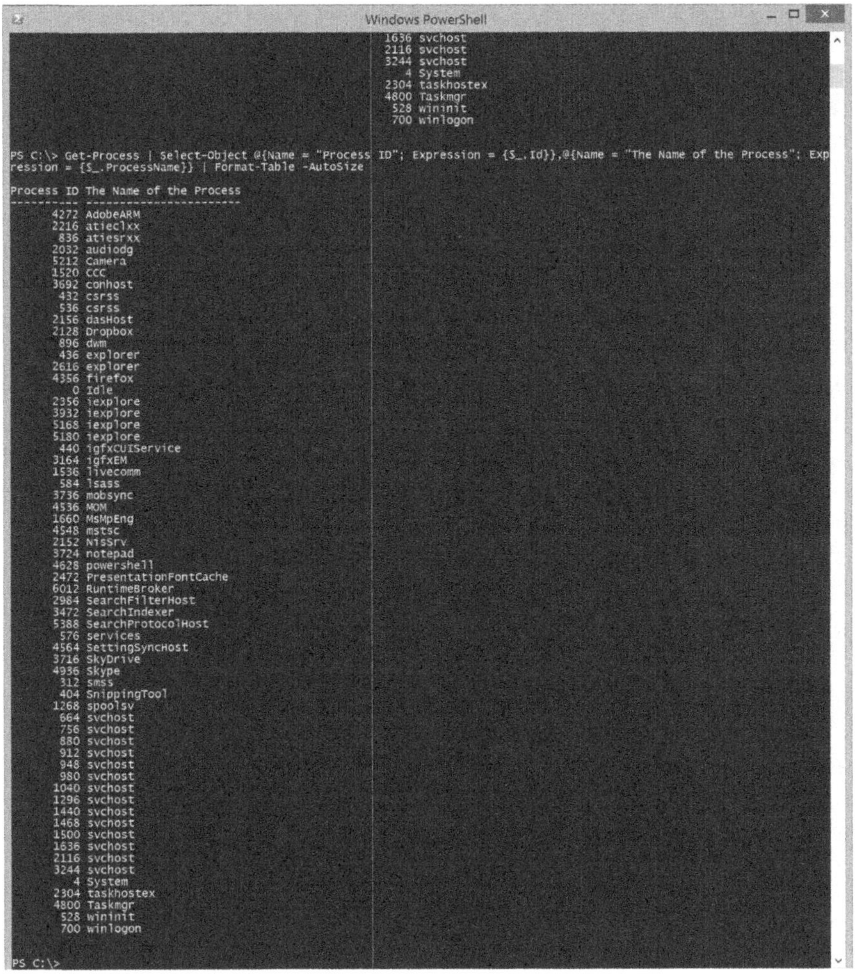

Figure 8.13: Using a hash table, part finale.

Figure 8.13 shows the final result. Pretty cool, huh? And now you see what I mean when I say the syntax is unforgiveable. But that is how PowerShell works, at least as the state of its art right now.

When might this be useful, however? There are some commands, particularly those that import data and need values named certain ways. But sometimes you might have data you need to import into those commands that is named in a different way. For instance, let's say you have a file that has a list of new interns that need accounts on your Active Directory domain. This might be a CSV feed from your hiring system, so it looks something like this:

```
First Name,Last Name,Logon Name,Division
Shelly,Johnson,sjohnson,Administrative
Brian,Smith,bsmith,Finance
Bridget,Williams,bwilliams,Communications
```

But when you try to create a new Active Directory Domain Services user account with PowerShell, you are confronted with the following problem: for the command that you will use, New-ADUser, there are parameters for GivenName and Surname and SamAccountName and Department. That's all well and good, but your file has data for First Name, Last Name, Logon Name, and Division. We'll use a hash table, then, with Select-Object to take care of renaming the headers in your CSV file to the names that New-ADUser is expecting. Finally, we'll pipe that into New-ADUser to finish up the job.

```
Import-CSV c:\interns.csv | Select-Object @{Name="Sur-
name";Expression={$_."Last Name"}},
@{Name="GivenName";Expression={$_."First Name"}},
@{Name="SamAccountName";Expression={$_."Logon Name"}},
@{Name="Department";Expression={$_."Division"}}
```

That was pretty in the weeds, wasn't it? But it's a very powerful capability and one you will surely use as you step into more advanced scripting and administration scenarios. In fact, I'll use it in the next section.

PowerShell in the Real World: Grouping and Comparing Objects

Now it's time to take all of this together and do something practical with all of your newfound knowledge. In this example, we will kick it up a notch and combine a lot of concepts we have discussed throughout this book, not just this chapter, to get at a common problem and provide a solution.

Let's say, purely hypothetically of course, that you have a ton of Exchange distribution groups. These are typically set up for projects, for organizational communications (so you'll have groups like "Sandra's Direct Reports" and "Accounting" and "Project Alpha Developers"), and then you might even have employee-directed social groups like "Foodies Unite!" or "Crazy Tacky Sweater Fridays" or anything similar. In all honesty, if your business has been around a few years and you have been running Exchange for any length of time, you probably have a number of these. Too many. And so you want to clean them up and decommission them so that your Global Address List (GAL) is smaller and loads quicker, while being easier to browse because there are fewer distribution lists.

Now, you do not want to make enemies, so you want to get rid of only distribution groups that have not been used in a while. You might want to set that limit at, say, three months. Any distribution group that has not had a single message processed to it in the past three months is a candidate for the trash heap. How can we use PowerShell to find a list of these groups and remove them?

Let's put on our scripting hat and think about how we might accomplish this task. I see it happening in three phases.

1. First, we need to get all of the distribution groups that are available to us.
2. We need to see which distribution lists have been used over the past 90 days (that is our three-month interval).
3. We'll then overlay the list of active distribution groups (in other words, those that *have* in fact been used) with the list of total distribution groups, and the ones that do not appear in both lists would be the inactive ones (in other words, the ones in the master list of all groups that don't also appear in the list of groups that have had activity in the past 90 days) and the groups that we can safely delete.

So let's begin with the commands. Now, unlike the rest of the book, I'm not going to give you a lesson in managing Exchange through PowerShell. I'm just going to come right out with the proper commands, because (a) not everyone has an Exchange box to test with and (b) not everyone needs to manage Exchange with

PowerShell. But with your knowledge so far, you should be able to follow along with my thought process, while looking at the structure of the commands and see exactly what each one is doing. You can then use this sort of "template" or this prime example to modify for your own uses. The bottom line: don't fret if you are not an Exchange administrator, but walk with me here as I explain what I am doing so that you can see the way I would approach this problem.

I'll be building the commands as I go along, and then at the end I'll present the complete code. You can run each of these as we go along, but there will be some duplication. That's still a good way to learn. Just don't get confused, as I want to show you *how* I'm approaching this problem and building these commands.

First, let's tackle phase one. I would need to find a command to *get* the *distribution group* entries that I have within Exchange.

```
Get-DistributionGroup
```

But what common element of distribution groups could we use to compare active groups? The e-mail address would be easiest. We're just a pipe and a Get-Member away from figuring out that PrimarySMTPAddress is the property name of the e-mail address for all distribution groups, so let's pipe the output of Get-DistributionGroup over to Select-Object to strip out the rest of the gunk.

```
Get-DistributionGroup | Select-Object PrimarySMTPAddress
```

Then we can just sort by that same property with a further pipe in order to get a nice, neat list.

```
Get-DistributionGroup | Select-Object PrimarySMTPAddress | Sort-Object PrimarySMTPAddress
```

Next, we need to get this information off of our screen and into a file. What could we use to write a table to a file useful for comparisons? I'd say Export-CSV.

```
Get-DistributionGroup | Select-Object PrimarySMTPAddress | Sort-Object PrimarySMTPAddress | Export-CSV allgroups.csv -notype
```

Phase one complete!

Then, I would need to find the list of distribution groups that have had activity over the past 90 days. There is a feature of Exchange called Message Tracking that writes out to message-tracking logs stored on the shared volume of the Exchange machine. From an Exchange machine, I could run `Get-Command -noun *Tracking*` and among some of the results, I would find `Get-MessageTrackingLog`. I would then run `Get-Help Get-MessageTrackingLog` to understand the parameters and the syntax available to me. I could also run `Show-Command Get-MessageTrackingLog` from the console to bring up the GUI window I could use to figure out the syntax and which parameters, if any, were required. After some of that research I just described, I could come out with the following command:

```
Get-MessageTrackingLog -Server EXCHANGE -EventId Expand -ResultSize Unlimited
```

But then I need to figure out how to sort that by e-mail addresses, so I use `Get-Member` and look at the output of `Get-MessageTrackingLog` to see what makes sense. I settle on the `RelatedRecipientAddress` property, so I pipe my original command to `Sort-Object` by that property:

```
Get-MessageTrackingLog -Server EXCHANGE -EventId Expand -ResultSize Unlimited | Sort-Object RelatedRecipientAddress
```

Then I'll group by that resulting object to control data output, in this case to aggregate the data by the recipient's e-mail address:

```
Get-MessageTrackingLog -Server EXCHANGE -EventId Expand -ResultSize Unlimited | Sort-Object RelatedRecipientAddress | Group-Object RelatedRecipientAddress
```

Then we'll do more sorting of the resulting object, this time by name:

```
Get-MessageTrackingLog -Server EXCHANGE -EventId Expand -ResultSize Unlimited | Sort-Object RelatedRecipientAddress | Group-Object RelatedRecipientAddress | Sort-Object Name
```

Now we'll create a little hash table goodness to rewrite the object output from here into something that `Compare-Object` would understand. The `RelatedRecipientAddress` property, which is now `Name`, should turn into `PrimarySMTPAddress` so that a proper, syntatically valid comparison can take place.

```
Get-MessageTrackingLog -Server EXCHANGE -EventId Ex-
pand -ResultSize Unlimited | Sort-Object RelatedRecip-
ientAddress | Group-Object RelatedRecipientAddress |
Sort-Object Name | Select-Object @{label=Prima-
rySmtpAddress;expression={$_.Name}}, Count
```

Now we just need to get that out to a CSV via one final pipe command.

```
Get-MessageTrackingLog -Server EXCHANGE -EventId Ex-
pand -ResultSize Unlimited | Sort-Object RelatedRecip-
ientAddress | Group-Object RelatedRecipientAddress |
Sort-Object Name | Select-Object @{label=Prima-
rySmtpAddress;expression={$_.Name}}, Count | Export-
CSV activegroups.csv -notype
```

Phase two complete!

Onto the final phase, where we actually perform the comparison. Our first order of business in this phase will be to get both CSV files into memory as objects by using variables.

```
$listofallgroups = Import-CSV allgroups.csv
$listofactivegroups = Import-CSV activegroups.csv
```

Then, we'll do a simple `Compare-Object` at first.

```
Compare-Object $listofallgroups $listofactivegroups -
Property PrimarySmtpAddress
```

Let's sort by e-mail address for a better, closer look:

```
Compare-Object $listofallgroups $listofactivegroups -
Property PrimarySmtpAddress | Sort-Object Prima-
rySmtpAddress
```

Now we'll select the addresses that are presented since they are the differences (the ones we want):

```
Compare-Object $listofallgroups $listofactivegroups -
Property PrimarySmtpAddress | Sort-Object Prima-
rySmtpAddress | Select-Object -Property PrimarySmtpAd-
dress
```

We're almost there! And now we'll write this to disk in a CSV format. What's getting written is the difference between all and active groups, which by defintion would be the inactive groups.

```
Compare-Object $listofallgroups $listofactivegroups -
Property PrimarySmtpAddress | Sort-Object Prima-
rySmtpAddress | Select-Object -Property PrimarySmtpAd-
dress | Export-Csv inactivegroups.csv -NoType
```

Nicely done! We've completed our task.
   As promised, here's the full script.

```
Get-DistributionGroup | Select-Object PrimarySMTPAd-
dress | Sort-Object PrimarySMTPAddress | Export-CSV
allgroups.csv -notype

Get-MessageTrackingLog -Server EXCHANGE -EventId Ex-
pand -ResultSize Unlimited | Sort-Object RelatedRecip-
ientAddress | Group-Object RelatedRecipientAddress |
Sort-Object Name | Select-Object @{Name=PrimarySmtpAd-
dress;Expression={$_.Name}}, Count | Export-CSV ac-
tivegroups.csv -notype

$listofallgroups = Import-CSV allgroups.csv
$listofactivegroups = Import-CSV activegroups.csv

Compare-Object $listofallgroups $listofactivegroups -
Property PrimarySmtpAddress | Sort-Object Prima-
rySmtpAddress | Select-Object -Property PrimarySmtpAd-
dress | Export-Csv inactivegroups.csv -NoType
```

The Last Word

Holy cow. That was a long chapter, but we covered a great deal of information about further working with objects, including how to compare two objects, select objects and certain properties about those objects, group objects together that share values, create hash tables and dynamically rewrite property names right within the pipeline so that data can be piped from one command to another command, and more. I also tied it up in a neat bow for you with the Exchange distribution group example.

Onward!

Chapter 9
To the Many, To the Few - PowerShell Remoting

Welcome to Chapter 9 of *Learning PowerShell*.

Imagine a scenario in which you have gained an appropriate level of PowerShell mastery and now you want to carry out your shelling wizardry and command line sorcery on other machines. What if I told you that I could have you in this new car for low payments of $169 a month?

Oh wait, wrong book.

What if I told you that you can use a couple of awesome PowerShell features to carry out as many commands as you want, even scripts, on up to 32 machines at a time? Can you imagine the things you could do to the systems you manage if you could run commands on all of them from a single console?

That's the power of remoting. Let's take a look and you'll see what I mean.

Introducing Remoting

Aside from what you can actually do with PowerShell on a single system, meaning the types of rote and repetitive tasks you can carry out with a command or two that would otherwise have required VBScript or Chinese torture camp-style manual labor, remoting is the coolest and most powerful feature of PowerShell.

One of the biggest criticisms of Windows in the enterprise for years has been levied by UNIX and Linux administrators regarding command-line administration of remote systems. Barely a day used to go by without a Linux guy saying to a Windows guy, "Where's your equivalent of SSH?" SSH is a secure shell environment commonly used by Linux, UNIX, BSD, and all the other *nix products. It essentially lets you replicate a terminal environment on your system. You can remote into other systems from the comfort of your own system, whether your target is under your desk, down the hall in the server room, or across the world in Russia. It is a very powerful feature, kind of like Telnet but on steroids and much more secure. For a while the only answer Windows had to such a management tool was Remote Desktop.

Of course, it is tough to script Remote Desktop, since you have to point and click with a mouse or touchpad in the GUI. And while Windows had a Telnet client and server, it was not installed by default, it was not secure, and it was not useful, as there were not many touch points exposed that the Windows version of Telnet could use to manage various facets of the operating system. And while you could use Remote Desktop to gain access to a system and fire off batch files

DOI 10.1515/9781501506673-009

and Visual Basic scripts, you still had to log in to the system visually first and, as far as I know, there was no way to do that automatically.

So, for workstations and employee desktops, folks generally shelled out tens of thousands of dollars for agent-based and WMI-based management suites such as System Center Configuration Manager, Solarwinds, or some other such products. For servers, while some used System Center to get those going as well, most just used good old-fashioned template-based imaging to build out the server in the first place and then super old-fashioned Remote Desktop to all the machines to complete, for example, ongoing maintenance tasks.

But now, there is an enterprise-class solution that affords you all the power of PowerShell with the ability to run all its commands from the command line on remote computers. It's called PowerShell remoting.

How Remoting Works

PowerShell remoting is predicated on two technologies: Web Services for Management, known as WSMan; and Windows Remote Management, or WinRM. The two technologies work in lockstep, with WSMan being the way commands are transmitted and WinRM providing the link between the network wire and PowerShell's command structure on all of the machines in question.

WSMan uses HTTP and HTTPS, the same protocols that the web operates on. It does this because (a) these technologies are well known and understood and (b) most firewalls already know how to inspect these types of communications, so it is not a special protocol that you have to enable. Compatibility is key in this scenario because obviously, you just want to be able to "spray" as many commands to as many remote computers as you can without having to worry about special protocols, firewall exceptions, opening nonstandard ports, and going over the security implications of yet another management technology. So WSMan carries the remoting commands between computers on the wire.

Once WSMan delivers the commands remotely, WinRM takes over. WinRM knows how to receive incoming PowerShell commands and in fact even understands more than just PowerShell. WinRM is now a preferred way for a lot of Microsoft applications to send information, commands, and input and output to various machines over the network. WinRM handles this by creating various *endpoints* on a system, which are basically like ports registered to a specific application. PowerShell creates an endpoint on a system when you enable remoting, but in actuality you can create multiple PowerShell endpoints on a system and restrict the scope of commands that can be run on any given endpoint, as well as restrict the computers or user accounts that can connect to any specific endpoint.

Most of that is beyond the scope of this book, but the key point to remember is that WinRM creates endpoints with *listeners* that accept incoming PowerShell commands over HTTP from WSMan.

Enabling PowerShell Remoting

It is actually super simple to enable PowerShell remoting. Open a PowerShell console as an administrator and simply type in

```
Enable-PSRemoting
```

and watch what happens. You can see the result in Figure 9.1.

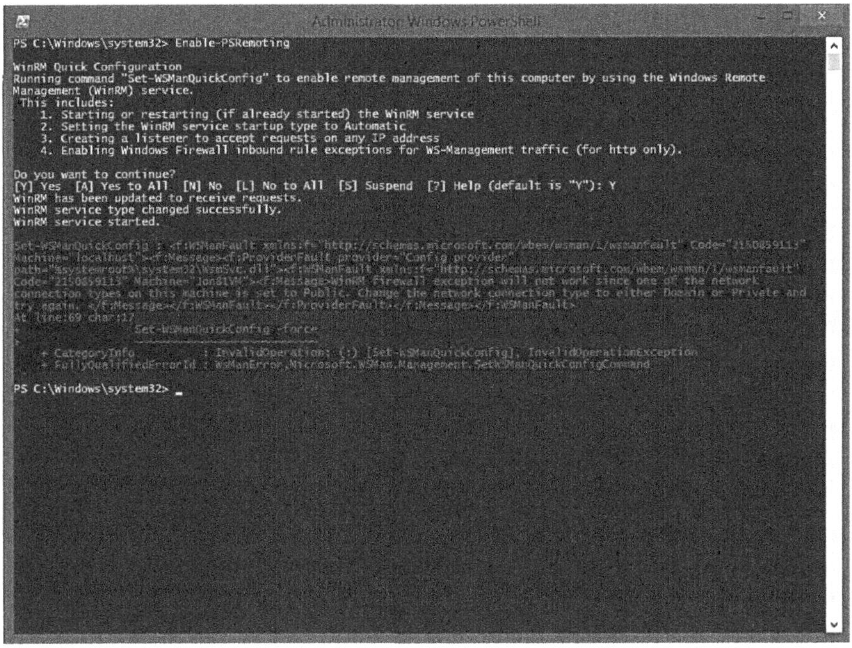

Figure 9.1: Attempting to enable PowerShell remoting with the `Enable-PSRemoting` command.

An error! If you look at the error message, it says, "Change the network connection type to either Domain or Private and try again." This is one of the most common error messages you will see, and it refers to the "network type" setting window that you may have seen pop up when you connect to a new wireless network. It will ask you what kind of network you are connecting to, and you can select between home or work, a domain network, or a private or public network. Here you need to select one of the trusted networks so that the remoting firewall exception for WSMan and WinRM can be set correctly.

Hopefully unsurprising to you at this point, given we are at Chapter 9 in this book, you can use PowerShell to get this done. Let's first get a look at the profile used by your network adapters:

```
Get-NetConnectionProfile
```

Look for the InterfaceIndex number of your wired or wireless (main) network adapter that is connected. Then, enter the following command, replacing `number` with that interface number as a numeric digit:

```
Set-NetConnectionProfile -InterfaceIndex number -NetworkCategory Private
```

You can then rerun `Enable-PSRemoting`. You must confirm four times that you want to enable various facets of the remoting experience. Just hit Y at the prompt to say "yes" and keep on. Rest assured knowing that only members of the administrators group can use remoting by default. You'd have to explicitly grant other users permissions for them to use remoting, so you can generally blow past these confirmation messages and still get a secure end state by default.

Remoting to One Computer at a Time

Remoting to one computer at a time is the equivalent of Telnetting or SSHing to a remote computer. You use your company and you target one other computer. By remoting to one computer, you are creating a PowerShell *session* to that computer, and any commands that you run will execute on that computer, and the results will show on the console screen of your local computer. It is a real-time connection and everything you see is actually happening on the remote computer. Think Remote Desktop, but without the GUI, just the command line. Your console and keyboard turn into extensions of the remote computer that you are targeting.

All you have to do to establish this *one-to-one remoting* session is to use the following command:

```
Enter-PSSession -computername TARGETCOMPUTER
```

Obviously, you would replace TARGETCOMPUTER with the full NetBIOS computer name of the remote computer you wish to use. To *exit* a *session* after you have entered it, you would use Exit-PSSession to close out your connection.

Once the session is established, you'll note that the prompt inside the console window changes to

```
[TARGETCOMPUTER] PS C:\Windows\System32\
```

This is your visual cue that you are operating in a remoting session. Your current credentials carry over to that machine, since PowerShell passes them along as Kerberos tickets and values.

That's all there is to it. For all intents and purposes, you are using the remote machine from your machine. Commands will work as if you were sitting in front of the remote machine. There is nothing more to explain here.

Remoting to Many Computers at a Time

The real power of PowerShell remoting comes with the ability to run a command on multiple computers simultaneously, all from the cozy comfort of your warm, dimly lit office. Wait, that's just me who has a dimly lit office?

There is a technical name for sending a command to multiple hosts at one time, at least in PowerShell lingo: *one-to-many remoting.* But you can kind of think of it as having your own little botnet, except you use your powers for good and not for evil.

You can make this magic happen with one little command, and this time I won't even make you hunt the help files and Get-Command for it. The phrase you are looking for is Invoke-Command, and it basically lets you *invoke* a com-*mand* on, by default, as many as 32 computers at one time.

The syntax is actually fairly easy to understand, especially in the relative framework and spectrum of PowerShell. You simply call Invoke-Command, then add a parameter called -ComputerName, add the computer or computers that you want to use, call another parameter called -scriptblock, and then add a left curly brace ({) and then the PowerShell command you want to execute on all of the computers you specified.

Here are some examples:

```
Invoke-Command -ComputerName JON-OFFICE -scriptblock {
Get-Process }
Invoke-Command -ComputerName SALESPC,ACCOUNTINGPC,RECE
PTIONPC -scriptblock { Get-EventLog -LogName Applicati
on -Newest 5}
```

There are a few key bits here to understand:

– **Difference between the `-ComputerName` parameter of any other command.** You will find throughout PowerShell some commands that are able to
accept multiple computer names as part of their native parameter set. This
type of command actually does not use remoting, and instead treats that set
as a sequential list. It will contact each computer through some method, basically whatever the .NET Framework chooses to use at the time, execute the
command, grab the output and mix it together with the other output, and
then move on to the next computer. This is no parallel processing. But it does
return real objects, which remoting itself using the `Invoke-Command` command does not always do. (More about that later in this chapter.) This is
something to keep in mind.

With a few exceptions, it is almost always more *efficient* in terms of processing
power and network bandwidth to use remoting to carry out commands on multiple machines than to use the serial processing power of the commands that accept multiple computers as part of their native parameter set. Some of the capabilities are different, so you may have a need to choose one over the other, but if
you only care about efficiency, all else being equal, remoting is the clear choice.

– **Running as an administrator.** You pretty much have to run as an administrator. For the remote computer, you can use the `-Credential` parameter
of `Invoke-Command` to specify an account with administrative privileges
on your target machine.

– **Specifying multiple computers.** When you are specifying more than one
computer on which to run commands as part of `Invoke-Command`'s `-`
`ComputerName` parameter, be sure to separate the computer names with a
comma and no spaces. You will want to use the full NetBIOS names of machines, not aliases via DNS, because PowerShell chokes on the DNS alias part
of things.

– **Understanding nested curly braces.** The content within the curly braces is
the command that will get executed on the remote machine or machines. If
that command has curly braces within it, be sure to understand how they nest

and remember all of the necessary right curly braces to close off the expressions, or you will receive syntax errors that can be maddening to troubleshoot and figure out.

— **The 32-computer invocation limit.** PowerShell by default throttles the command to invoke other commands to 32 computers at a time, mainly because most networks can't handle the bandwidth to serialize and deserialize communications with that many computers simultaneously (otherwise known as *in parallel*), and because you probably are not equipped to deal interactively with that many responses coming at you so quickly. If you specify more than 32 computers, PowerShell will queue up computers number 33 and above and wait for responses to come in from the first 32 computers before moving along down the line.

— **Reaching out to more than 32 computers.** If you are a heavy hitter administrator and you need to run commands on more than 32 computers at a time and have the network bandwidth to do so, you can use the `-ThrottleLimit` parameter to extend the goodness. Just type in the number of computers that you want to hit after the parameter, and don't forget the space between the parameter name and its value.

— **How commands are executed**. The one in one-to-many doesn't just apply to the local machine. It also applies to the number of commands or script blocks a single `Invoke-Command`-based remoting session can handle. That's one. What actually happens is that PowerShell.exe, the console host, is called on each remoting session on the remote computer. It opens up, executes the command, does its serialization and deserialization routine, and then shuts down. The next remoting command opens up a fresh new instance of PowerShell.exe. So, in remoting, there is no history, the variables you declare expire, and everything is very transient.

Specifying a Script File Instead of a Command

You might be interested in running a full script on a remote computer or set of machines via the `Invoke-Command` feature. That might be a script with four or five commands, or just a couple of commands with some gnarly syntax or a couple of hash tables that might get entered incorrectly if you were to type them over again at the command line. Luckily, there is the `-FilePath` parameter that you can use instead of the `-scriptblock` parameter. With `-FilePath` you simply specify the script file on your local system that you want to use to execute on the remote computers. Remember, of course, that a PowerShell script file is simply a text file saved with the .ps1 extension.

Specifying a Separate List of Computers

You might also want to run commands on a list of computers you have developed from some other source. Maybe another command you ran wrote some output to a file that is a list of computers that meet some conditions; maybe your automated management software suite put out a list of computers that need some administrative task carried out on them; or something else. You can work a list of computers that is in a text file, one on each line with no other formatting, into the `Invoke-Command` command by simply enclosing the `Get-Content` command with the text file specified in parenthesis as the value of the `-ComputerName` parameter for `Invoke-Command`.

Let's look at an example of this. Let's say I have a list of client machines in my text file that I suspect may have been compromised by some sort of security breach. I want to get the newest 20 entries in their security event log and get all those results returned to me. I would create that text file like so:

```
CLIENT1
CLIENT10
ACCOUNTINGPC
ENGINEERING9
REMOTE2
```

I would save it as clients.txt. You see I have done nothing special there except write each computer's NetBIOS name on a separate line. I do not need column headers, commas, semicolons, or any other sort of formatting.

Next, I'll use `Invoke-Command` and write my code.

```
Invoke-Command -scriptblock { Get-EventLog -LogName
Security -Newest 20 } -computername
```

You'll see I stopped there, without specifying a value for `-ComputerName`. That's because I want to use `Get-Content` to read in the values of the clients.txt file that have my list of selected hosts. I'll just encompass this in parentheses to reflect that it is a separate operation, and I will be good to go.

```
Invoke-Command -scriptblock { Get-EventLog -LogName
Security -Newest 20 } -computername (Get-Content cli-
ents.txt)
```

The Caveats When Using Remote Commands

Make no mistake: the remoting feature is extremely powerful, but that does not mean that executing remote commands using `Invoke-Command` has an exact, 100%, one-to-one match experience- and feature-wise with using local commands. There are a couple of reasons why, and it all has to do with how commands are sent from your local machine to the remote machine, and how the remote machine executes the commands and sends the output back over the wire to your local machine.

Serialization and Deserialization Side Effects

The biggest difference is in the output that your local machine receives from each computer you "remote" to execute commands. As part of the transmission process, your local machine *serializes* the command you send, which basically means PowerShell turns your command into an XML file that can traverse over HTTP, basically like a web page. The remote machine is configured to accept and read these XML files, and then it converts the command from the XML format back into PowerShell's native format and executes the command. After the command has finished running, PowerShell converts the output back into XML (another *serialization*) and then returns the file to our local machine. Our local machine then *deserializes* that XML transmission into what are probably best known as pseudoobjects.

Why am I using the term pseudoobjects? Because they act like objects in some ways, but they aren't exactly real objects of the type you would expect to be returned from running any given command locally via the PowerShell console. Let's take our tried and true example, `Get-EventLog -LogName Application -Newest 5`. If I ran that locally, you know by now that what will be returned is a collection of five event log objects, one for each entry. Those objects will have all the properties, members, and events you would expect from a standard event log object. But if I run `Get-EventLog -LogName Application -Newest 5` remotely, then what I get back are:

— **objects that have a new property you won't find locally.** That property is called `PSComputerObject,` and it includes the name of the computer on which the command was run, so you can easily tag the returned object to the computer that put it out. Not so helpful if you are remoting one to one, but if you have a list of 64 computers, you might want to know which objects came from which of those 64 machines.

— **results from a snapshot, or a state in time.** Think of yourself standing in the middle of a European train station or a big American airport like Dallas-Fort Worth or Chicago. Someone from your home office asks to know which flights or trains are delayed. Rather than type them out one by one, you take a photo of the departures board with your smartphone and e-mail or text it back to the person asking for it. That photo contains a lot of trains or flights and their statuses, but the statuses are from the time that you took the photo. In the interim, perhaps the airline brings in another aircraft to replace a ship that was not in sound mechanical order, and as such a delayed flight can leave earlier than indicated. Unless you take another photo of the departures board or otherwise notify the person back in your home office, he or she will not receive that information, because all that person has is a snapshot of flight or train statuses at the exact instance you took the picture. Running a command remotely via remoting is exactly the same way. If you are asking for the newest 5 event log entries, then what you will get back are the newest 5 event log entries *at the time the command was run.*

There is one other caveat to speak about, and that involves pipeline processing when you want to do more than just format or export data. Many times, the serialization and deserialization process loses some vital information about the computers responsible for any command's output and objects. Because of this, many folks try to do actions to deserialized objects that come back from a remoting session and they see that they fail. For instance, if you are trying to stop a process on a remote computer, you might try to use some command like:

```
Invoke-Command -scriptblock { Get-Process chrome } -
computername CLIENT1 | Stop-Process
```

We can step through this. PowerShell will serialize the command, translate it into XML, and send `Get-Process chrome` over to the remote computer. The remote computer will execute the command, serialize the output, convert it to XML, and then return it to your local machine. Your local machine will deserialize the output, convert it to regular PowerShell, and then pipe it to

```
Stop-Process...
```

...and your local machine will raise its eyebrows at you and say to you in its dumbest voice, "Huh? I don't have a process called chrome." What has happened here? What's happened is that there is not enough information in that output returned from your remote machine to tell `Stop-Process` that the `chrome` value it is receiving is actually from a remote computer. So, your local computer is looking for a process that does not exist on your local computer because it has no idea that the process is running remotely. It has no way to connect back to that remote computer to execute the stop part of your wishes even if it were smart enough to know.

The lesson here is to always do as much as your command as you can on your remote machines. A simple change to the above command, like...

```
Invoke-Command -scriptblock { Get-Process chrome |
Stop-Process } -computername CLIENT1
```

...would complete successfully, because everything is running remotely (everything is within the curly braces of the script block so the whole thing gets sent over the wire to be executed on your target machine).

A good rule of thumb is that if you are doing anything *other than* formatting, converting, or exporting on your local machine as part of a remoting command, then you should do it all on the remote machine.

Remoting with Efficiency in Mind
Let's also talk for a minute about efficiency. If you are running commands remotely and attempting to do some logical processing on them using `Select-Object` or `Where-Object` on your local machine, stop and think for a moment. Wouldn't it be better for that sorting and filtering and limiting to be done on each remote machine with using the big set of original objects from only that machine? Otherwise, you would have a scenario where you are grabbing, say, 5,000 event log entries from 32 computers, so 5,000 x 32 = 160,000 event log entries would be shipped over the wire to your local machine, wasting network bandwidth, and then your poor local machine would have to do the pipeline processing on 160,000 objects. Instead, it would absolutely be more efficient to do the pipeline processing on each of the 32 machines out there, and have them ship back only the results that pass through your sorting or limiting or filtering. Much less work for your local machine, much less network bandwidth wasted, and much more distributed computing power, meaning many hands translate directly into lighter work.

Remoting Needs Some Permission Sometimes

In a regular domain environment where your local machine is a member of an Active Directory domain, and the target machines for your remoting efforts are members of the same Active Directory domain, you are pretty much golden. However, if you are remoting across different domains, there is a problem. As Ed Wilson, Microsoft's scripting guy, puts it, "The issue is that the client machine and the remote machine are not able to mutually authenticate as they would within a domain."

The solution is to add your local machine to the remote machine's trusted hosts list. It's an internal list that PowerShell keeps of machines it is used to and has been told to trust, and therefore PowerShell does not need to go through the mutual authentication checks that remoting typically requires.

One command will take care of this for you:

```
Set-item wsman:localhost\client\trustedhosts -value
RemotingLocalMachine1,RemotingLocalMachine2
```

An alternative for getting remoting in mixed domains working is to make a couple of Registry changes. Specifically, these changes to the remote machine let the client server to authenticate from a different domain, or with an account local to the remote server.

```
New-ItemProperty -name LocalAccountTokenFilterPolicy -
path HKLM:\SOFTWARE\Microsoft\Windows\CurrentVer-
sion\Policies\System -PropertyType DWORD -value 1
```

With this configuration, you need to call the `Get-Credential` command to capture your credentials, and then you use the `Invoke-Command` cmdlet's `-Credential` parameter to include that credential in your remoting request.

```
$credential = Get-Credential
Invoke-Command -ComputerName TARGETMACHINE -Script-
Block {your commands here} -Credential $credential
```

Alternatively, you can create the credential explicitly in script. This is a little in the weeds, but at this point you ought to be able to follow along with what I have done here.

```
$securePassword = ConvertTo-SecureString "pass-
word123letmein" -AsPlainText -force

$credential = New-Object System.Management.Automa-
tion.PsCredential("DOMAIN\username",$securePassword)

Invoke-Command -ComputerName TARGETMACHINE -Script-
Block {your commands here} -Credential $credential
```

I declared a variable to store the password, and then I used the command `Con-vertTo-SecureString` to hash up the plain text password that I put in quote marks. Then, I created the variable to hold the credentials and created a new PowerShell object of type `PSCredential` (this part is the advanced part that I fully expect you to simply gloss over, but I thought I would explain it anyway in case it got your creative juices and curiosity flowing) to store both my username, with domain specified, as well as my hashed up password from before. At that point, I just use the regular `Invoke-Command` command and put the variables where the syntax requires them.

The Last Word

Remoting is an amazing feature. Whether you are using one-to-one or one-to-many remoting to carry out your administrative tasks, you will find that PowerShell now is an enterprise-class, carrier=grade command line solution for managing multiple machines at a time. Imagine the power you now have at your fingertips.

Chapter 10
Useful PowerShell Tools

Welcome to Chapter 10 of *Learning PowerShell*!

Ah, PowerShell. A simple blue window and some text has transformed the world of Windows administration from a point-and-click GUI to scripts that automate everything, as well as provide log rotation and identify lifecycle management and which server receives which updates.

With everything in the newest versions of Windows Server accessible primarily via PowerShell and only secondarily (and sometimes even not at all) via the server's GUI, PowerShell knowledge has become a must. Sometimes, though, it is difficult to know whether you are proceeding correctly. Luckily, other available resources will help speed you along in your training and your professional responsibilities.

In this chapter, I will highlight nine resources for immersing yourself in the PowerShell world. Whether you're writing scripts, working in a DevOps-oriented environment or administering software from vendors other than Microsoft while using PowerShell, there is something for everyone in this group of resources. And best of all, they are all free, save for one excellent paid product.

What are you waiting for? Let's dive in.

Dell PowerGUI

Presumably left over from Dell's 2012 acquisition of Quest, PowerGUI is a visual complement to PowerShell. It makes assembling scripts and getting things done in PowerShell as simple as selecting cmdlets appropriate for your task and then dragging them into place. Perfect for those who are new to PowerShell but have a basic grasp of its concepts, PowerGUI is an easy-to-use script editor that will probably advance your understanding of assembling more complex and advanced scripts quicker than anything else—especially if you are a visual learner. Take a look at Figure 10.1.

DOI 10.1515/9781501506673-010

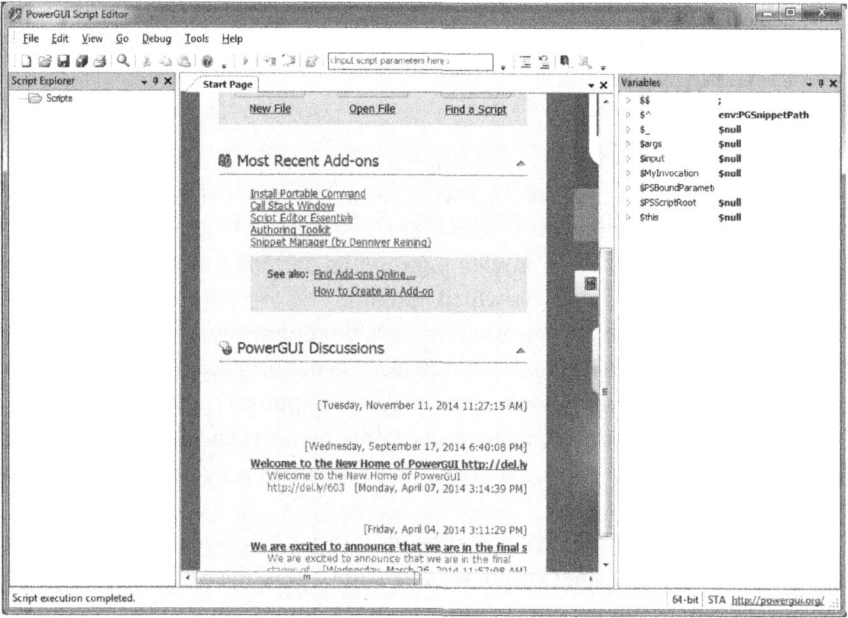

Figure 10.1: Dell PowerGUI.

Perhaps the most useful features of PowerGUI are the Power Packs: pre-built scripts that have been open-sourced by the user community and made available to other PowerGUI users. These range from adding users to managing switches; they can be customized and further improved upon, or simply baked into whatever script you are writing, saving the time it would take you to reinvent the wheel.

There was once a paid edition of PowerGUI with more advanced features, but that edition was rolled up into the freeware product. PowerGUI does not seem to have been updated for a while, but that does not make it any less useful, and since it is freeware, you have nothing to lose by adding it to your arsenal.

Freeware. http://software.dell.com/products/powergui-freeware/

SAPIEN Technologies PowerShell Studio 2015

More advanced PowerShell developers and administrators need more advanced tooling, and PowerShell Studio 2015 from Sapien is the first place to look. When you first open PowerShell Studio, as you can see from Figure 10.2, you are immediately reminded of Visual Studio and for good reason: PowerShell Studio is as much an integrated scripting environment as Visual Studio is an integrated development environment (IDE).

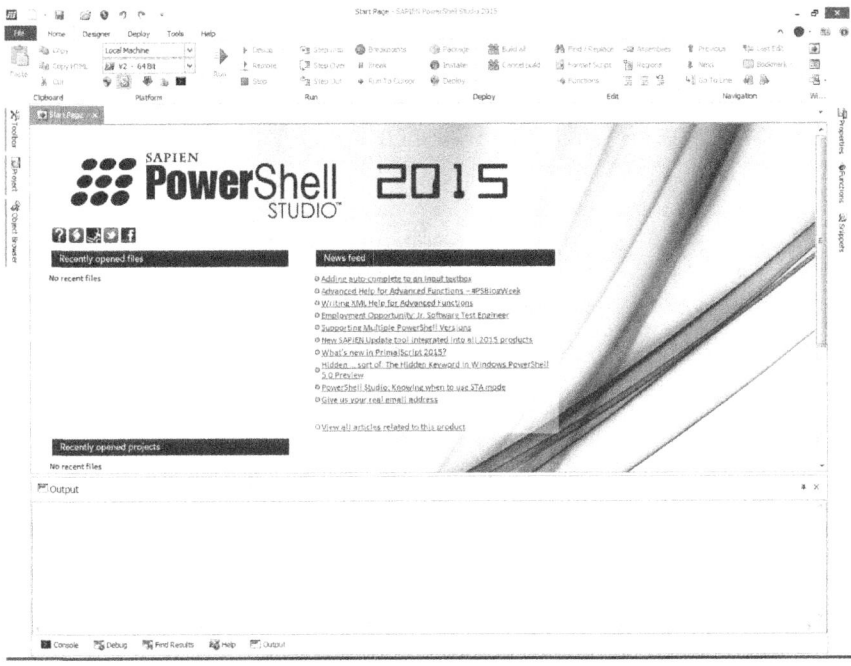

Figure 10.2: SAPIEN Technologies PowerShell Studio 2015.

Features include: ribbon, remote debugging support, compiler features that let you turn scripts into executable files, support for multiple versions of PowerShell (useful for targeting scripts to different servers running different levels of the Windows Server operating system), source control for checking in and out script code, and support for multiple developers. All of which make this an obvious choice for shops where administrators and developers work together on building advanced PowerShell scripts to handle a variety of scenarios.

At $389 per license, it is a little pricey. But considering all of the product's functionality, if you live in this part of the PowerShell world, it is well worth the cost of admission.

45-day free trial, $389 per license. http://www.sapien.com/software/ powershell_studio

Amazon AWS Tools for Windows PowerShell

It's not just Microsoft that is jumping on the PowerShell bandwagon; even a competitive cloud service like Amazon Web Services recognizes that (a) Windows Server is huge, (b) lots of administrators are learning PowerShell, and (c) anything that lets administrators manage Amazon services more easily increases the likelihood that an Amazon server will stick in any given enterprise. Thus, AWS Tools for Windows PowerShell was born—see the introduction in Figure 10.3.

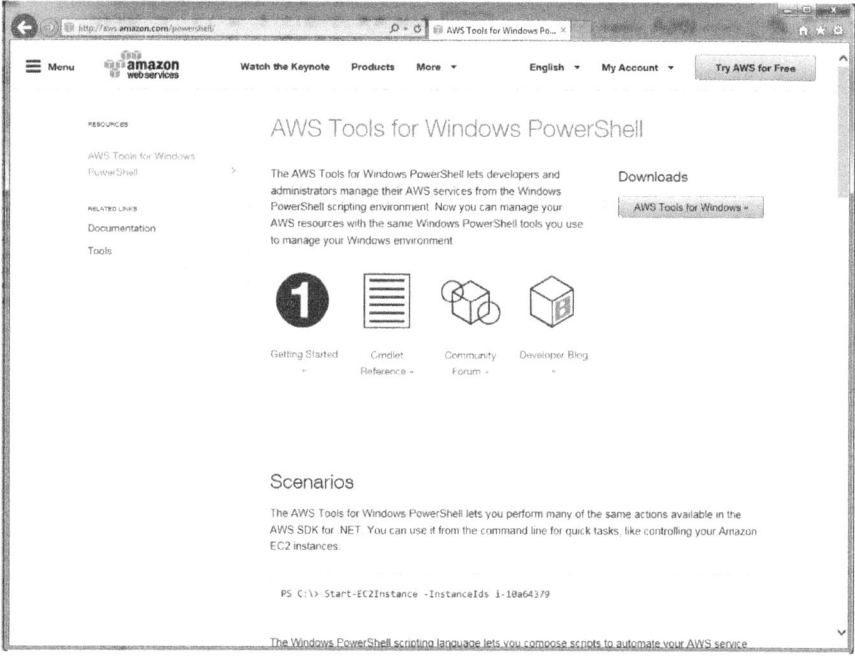

Figure 10.3: Amazon AWS Tools for Windows PowerShell.

With AWS Tools for Windows PowerShell, you can manage virtual machines and service instances running in the Elastic Compute Cloud (EC2), or write scripts that automate the management of any workloads you have running in a variety of Amazon services. The tools install a bunch of cmdlets into your Windows PowerShell "sphere of influence" and let you manage and script tasks like backing up data from virtual machines in EC2 to the Simple Storage Service (S3) or logging and publishing metrics to the Amazon CloudWatch personal dashboard.

If you know PowerShell and you use Amazon cloud services, these tools will be a great addition.

Freeware. http://aws.amazon.com/powershell/

Microsoft Script Browser for Windows PowerShell ISE

The problem: You want to do something in PowerShell. You know your outcome. But you do not know how to get there and, further, you have a sneaking suspicion that someone, somewhere out there on the Internet has already figured it out and probably would tell you for free. What if there were a free magic tool that would scour the TechNet Script Center—probably the most authoritative source for PowerShell scripts on Earth right now—and find scripts that purport to do what you need? That is exactly what Microsoft Script Browser (as shown in Figure 10.4) claims to do.

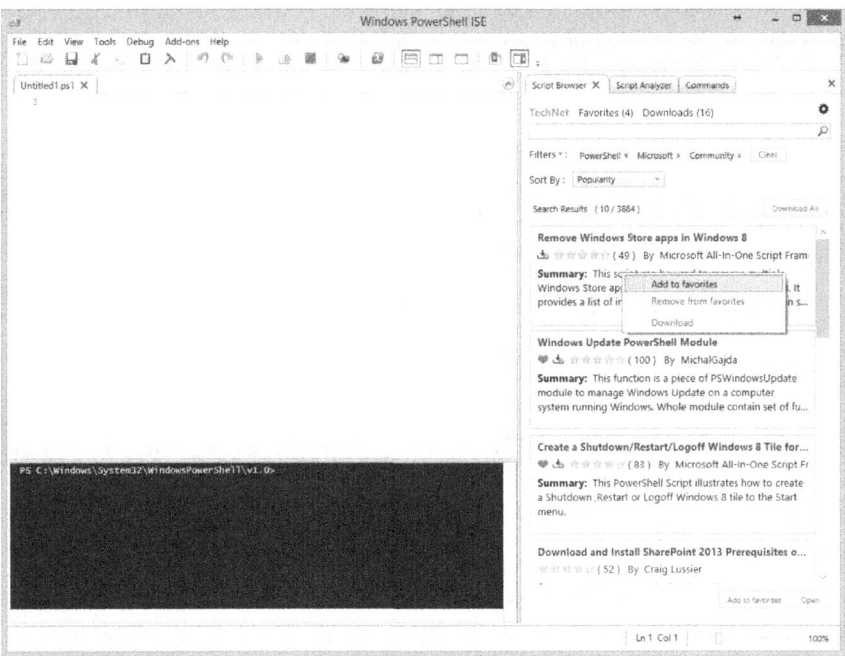

Figure 10. 4: Microsoft Script Browser for Windows PowerShell ISE.

It also includes a built-in Script Analyzer function that will read through your scripts and suggest improvements or changes to make based upon scripting best practices.

This tool plugs right into the Windows PowerShell Integrated Scripting Environment, which is free as part of Windows. You might need to install the feature on Windows client machines, but it should be installed by default as part of the basic Windows Server image.

Freeware, requires a Windows license and Windows PowerShell ISE to be installed. http://www.microsoft.com/ en-us/download/details.aspx? id=42525

Adam Driscoll's PowerShell Tools for Visual Studio

If you are more on the "dev" side of DevOps, then you probably use Visual Studio as one of your tools of choice. While Visual Studio has a lot going for it, it does not do a lot with PowerShell out of the box. That is where Adam Driscoll's PowerShell Tools for Visual Studio project, which you can see in Figure 10.5, comes in.

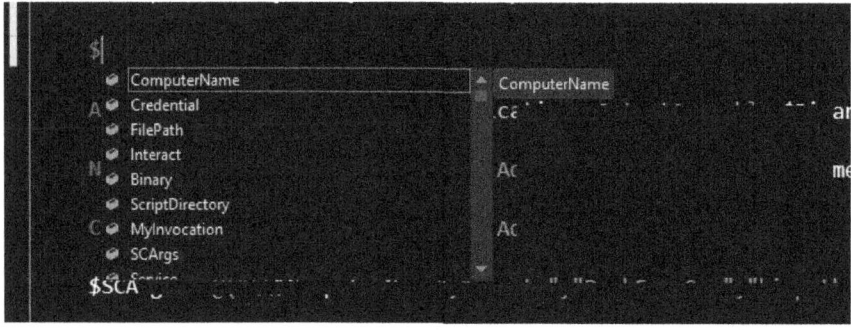

Figure 10.5: Adam Driscoll's PowerShell Tools for Visual Studio.

This project integrates within Visual Studio, brings syntax highlighting and colors to the IDE, and adds IntelliSense support for automatically completing syntax elements like variables, cmdlets and arguments as you type within a Visual Studio window. It also extends options for configuring Visual Studio projects so you can keep your scripting efforts organized and together, extends support for scripting arguments with the MS Build compiler, and supports script debugging via breakpoint and breakpoint pane support. It also extends some testing features with Pester and PSate test adapters.

All in all, this is a free set of resources for making Visual Studio more PowerShell savvy. If you like this after downloading it, consider throwing Mr. Driscoll a few bucks for his efforts.

Free, with donations solicited. http://adamdriscoll.github.io/poshtools/ Also from MSDN. https://visualstudiogallery.msdn.microsoft.com/c9eb3ba8-0c59-4944-9a62-6eee37294597

Microsoft Windows PowerShell Web Access, via Control Panel

PowerShell Web Access is like webmail but for PowerShell cmdlets—go ahead, peek at Figure 10.6 to see what I mean. You log in to a webpage that presents a web-based console where you can run cmdlets, perform operations, and do simple remote administration tasks right over the Internet. There's no need for PowerShell, extensions, or cmdlets to be installed on the machine you are browsing with.

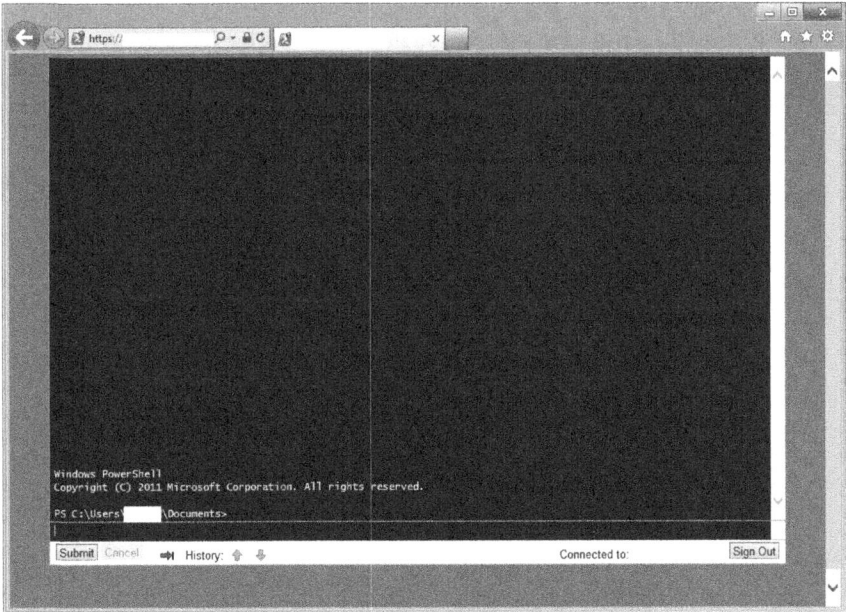

Figure 10.6: Microsoft Windows PowerShell Web Access, via Control Panel.

This means that, yes, you can run PowerShell operations from your iPad if you have this feature enabled.

Best of all, it is free with a Windows Server license and is built right in. I do not see this in use a lot, but I think it is very handy. As the saying goes, "You might not need this until you need it, but when you do end up needing it, you need it very badly."

Be careful, though, as opening this facility up to users outside your network is an invitation for security problems. Restrict access to the PowerShell Web Access site in IIS to only IP addresses local to your corporate network. Or even better, restrict that access to a few workstations on your local network and perhaps a static VPN address you can use to perform administration tasks remotely.

Free. Windows feature, installed through Control Panel / Add and Remove Windows Features. You can also check out Microsoft's help page on this. https://technet.microsoft.com/en-us/library/hh831611.aspx

PowerShell Training via the Microsoft Virtual Academy

With great power comes the need for a lot of training. PowerShell is a capable language that can do so much. It marries scripting with development and .NET programming. It comes with a universe of cmdlets. It has its own syntax. And while I have explained PowerShell basics in this book, I promise I have just barely scratched the surface of all there is to know.

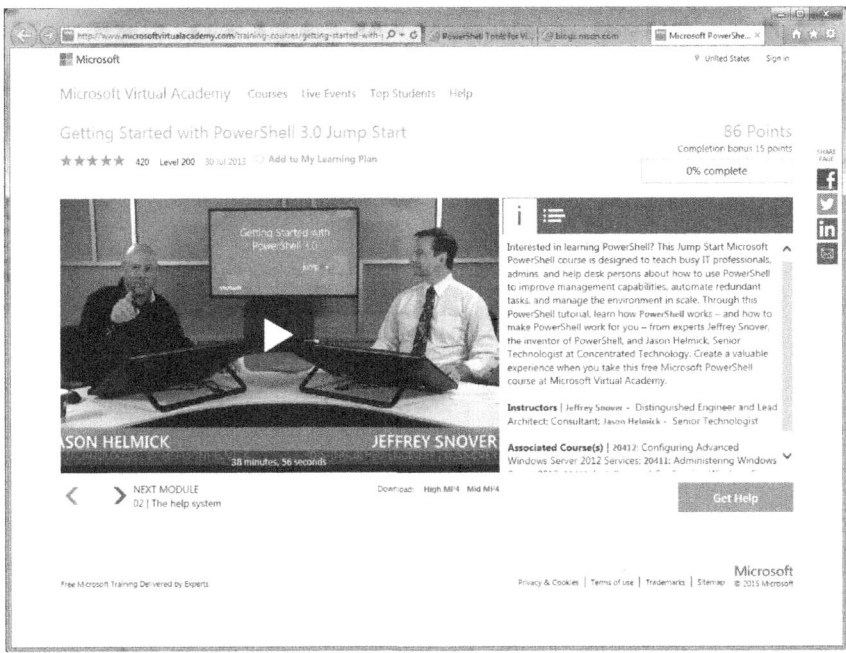

Figure 10.7: PowerShell Training via the Microsoft Virtual Academy.

Fortunately, the Microsoft Virtual Academy contains hours of video training, an example of which is shown in Figure 10.7, on getting to know PowerShell, using it, and making the language work for you. These courses include information from stars such as the father of PowerShell, Jeffrey Snover, and distinguished technologists who have made (new) careers out of understanding every nook and cranny of PowerShell. Perfect for lunch hours.

    Freeware. http://www.microsoftvirtualacademy.com/training-courses/ getting-started- with-powershell-3-0-jump-start

Master-PowerShell, an eBook from Dr. Tobias Weltner

If you are a visual learner, then video training is the best way to learn PowerShell. For those of us more language inclined, we can learn from Microsoft MVP Dr. Tobias Weltner in his free eBook, cleverly titled *Master-PowerShell*.

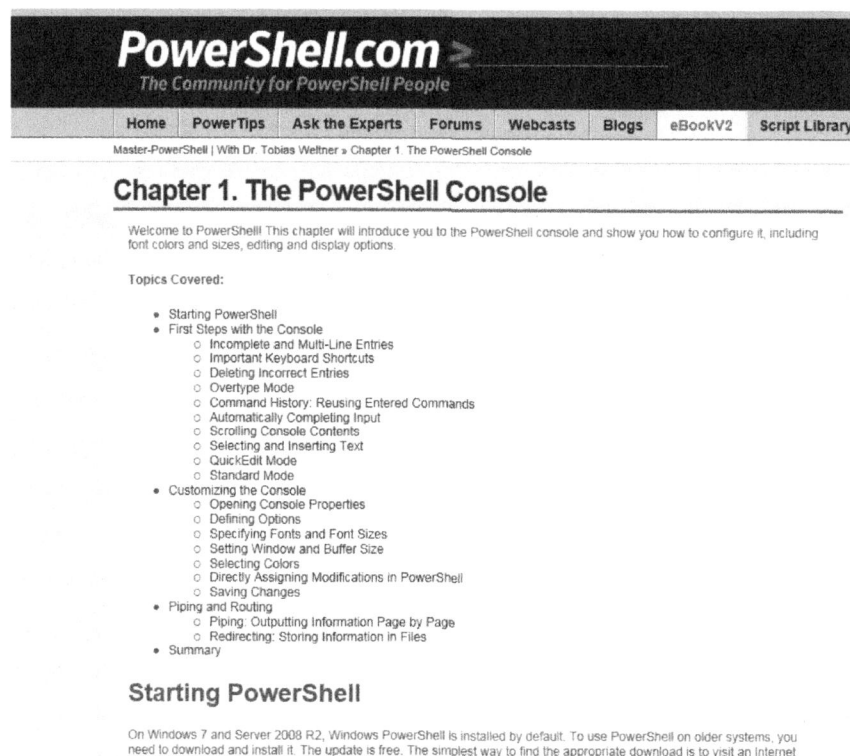

Figure 10.8: Master-PowerShell, an eBook from Dr. Tobias Weltner.

As you can see from Figure 10.8, Weltner covers a lot of ground in his book, including variables, arrays and hashtables, the pipeline, objects, conditions, loops, functions, scripts, error handling, scope, text and regular expressions. Also included: XML, administrative work using the file system, Registry, processes, services, event logs, WMI and users. He even includes a chapter on .NET and compiling for the developers among us.

The book is hosted by Idera, a popular administrative tool developer, and can be found on the PowerShell.com site, which is a useful community resource in its own right.

Free. http://powershell.com/cs/blogs/ebookv2/default.aspx

VMware vSphere PowerCLI

Like Amazon, VMware has figured out that, in some respects, making nice with your competitors for the benefit of your mutual customers is not a bad thing. To that end, VMware created PowerCLI, a command line-based environment shown in Figure 10.9 for managing VMware vSphere resources that integrates PowerShell throughout.

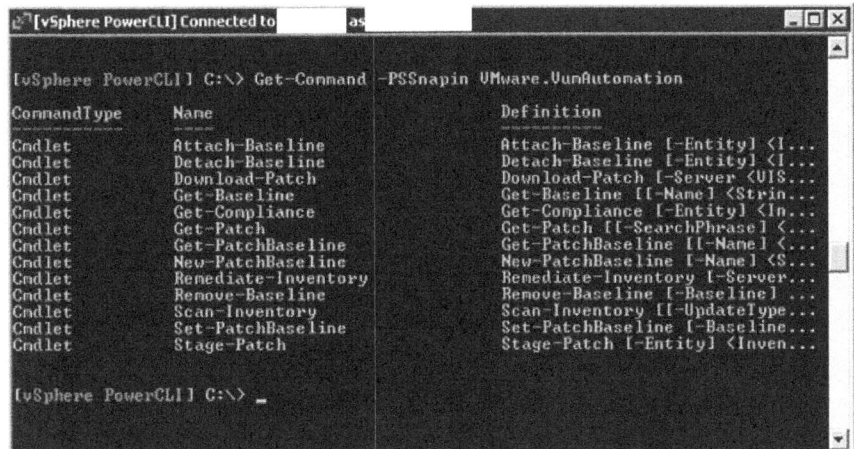

Figure 10.9: VMware vSphere PowerCLI.

The PowerCLI environment is basically a bunch of cmdlets that interact with vSphere and vCloud, and provides interfaces based on C# and PowerShell for the various APIs that are exposed by the VMware products. If you are a VMware shop and want to get your hands on PowerCLI, head over to this link: http://pubs.vmware.com/vsphere-60/index.jsp?topic=%252Fcom.vmware. powercli.cmdletref.doc%252FOverview.html&__utma=207178772.498640042.14 26176019.1426176019.1426176019.1&__utmb=207178772.0.10.1426176019&__utm c=207178772&__utmx=-&__utmz=207178772.1426176019.1.1.utmcsr=google%257 Cutmccn=%2528organic%2529%257Cutmcmd=organic%257Cutmctr=%2528not %20provided%2529&__utmv=-&__utmk=74503057

Is it not great when everyone plays nicely together in the sandbox?

Freeware, with a free cmdlet reference available.

https://www.vmware.com/ support/developer/PowerCLI/

The Last Word

There is a lot in the box when it comes to PowerShell, but that absolutely does not change the fact that Windows and Microsoft technologies in general have always had a rich ecosystem of partners and independent software vendors that enjoy taking the basics the software giant puts out there and extending them into better versions of themselves. The nine PowerShell tools I have profiled in this chapter do exactly that. They make PowerShell use easier, better, and more compatible with a wide variety of products and services that most of us see in our daily professional lives.

Onward!

Chapter 11
Using PowerShell to Manage Office 365

In this chapter of *Learning PowerShell*, I am going to try to put all the pieces together and show you some PowerShell in action. Lots of people don't realize you can do all sorts of administrative tasks with Office 365 outside of the web portal. You can set passwords, assign licenses, perform group maintenance, configure external sharing, perform retention holds and more, all with PowerShell and never touching the web browser. Here are 10 examples of PowerShell commands you can use to manage your Office 365 deployment. You'll notice that all these commands use techniques I have taught you in this book and course: they wrap up a lot of PowerShell features and functionality to really carry out some practical tasks!

Create a Script to Open a PowerShell Session to Office 365

It is kind of the way that it is, unfortunately, but to manage Office 365 through PowerShell you have to create a remote session to the Office 365 servers in order to run commands against the service, and sometimes that is a little clunky. Here I have a simple script that you can run to actually get yourself logged in and ready to roll.

```
$URL = "https://ps.outlook.com/powershell"
$Credentials = Get-Credential -Message "Enter your Ex-
change Online or Office 365 administrator credentials"
$CloudSession = New-PSSession -ConfigurationName Mi-
crosoft.Exchange -ConnectionUri $URL -Credential $Cre-
dentials -Authentication Basic -AllowRedirection -Name
"Office 365/Exchange Online"
Import-PSSession $CloudSession -Prefix 365
```

First, it defines the URL of the Office 365 servers as a variable, and then it also defines another variable to hold your credentials. That variable calls the Get-Credential command with a brief message explaining which credentials are needed, and it hashes and stores the results inside the variable. Then, I define the CloudSession variable, which contains the results of the New-PSSession cmdlet, which connects to the URL with the credentials stored in the $Creden-

DOI 10.1515/9781501506673-011

tials variable. Finally, it imports the remote PowerShell session and command namespace into the console and prefixes all of the remote commands with a 365 to avoid collisions with the local versions of those commands. This happens, for instance, in the case where you are managing, say, Exchange on premises as well as Office 365 remotely. Save this with a PS1 extension and run it whenever you need to connect to Office 365 to do some management, and you will save yourself time.

Assign Rights to Mailboxes

Often, a common task for administrators is to let someone else have access to another user's mailbox. That could be for the executive assistant to manage his director's e-mail account, or it could be for a group of users to be able to "send e-mail as" the account of a shared mailbox so that all replies are directed back to said shared mailbox so the team handles issues and messages centrally. PowerShell makes quick work of this.

For full access:

```
Add-MailboxPermission -identity themailboxinquestion -
user theuserwhoneedsaccesstothatmailbox -AccessRights
FullAccess -InheritanceType All
```

For send as permissions:

```
Set-Mailbox -Identity themailboxinquestion -
GrantSendOnBehalfTo theuserwhoneedstosendasthatmailbox
```

If you have a longer list of people who require access, then get those users into a variable and then send that variable to the command. For example:

```
$userswhoneedtosendas = Get-Mailbox OrganizationalUnit
CustomerService
Set-Mailbox -identity customerservice@yourorganiza-
tion.org -GrantSendOnBehalfTo $userswhoneedtosendas
```

Converting Regular Mailboxes to Shared Mailboxes

We all have to handle departing employees and users who for one reason or another separate from our organization. In traditional setups, we can keep mailboxes around for as long as we want to because there is no additional cost to keeping a user's mailbox active and accessible on a typical Exchange system. Within Office 365, however, any given user's mailbox is tied to a service license, which represents an actual recurring monthly cost, so it is in your organizations best interest to transition that mailbox as quickly as possible, enabling you to reassign the license to a new employee or cancel it and save the monthly cost.

You do this by converting an active mailbox to a shared mailbox, since the latter can exist without monthly license costs. Then you can assign full access or "send as" permissions as needed when you have to access the content stored in the departed employee's mailbox.

NOTE: Shared mailboxes can have only 5 GB of information in them. If your departed employee's mailbox has more than 5 GB, then you will need to pare it down before you can convert. You also will need the Azure Active Directory module for PowerShell, which you can find here: http://aka.ms/aadposh

---

First, change the mailbox type to convert the mailbox to a shared account:

```
Set-Mailbox -Identity departedemployee -Type Shared -
ProhibitSendReceiveQuota 5GB -ProhibitSendQuota 4.75GB
-IssueWarningQuota 4.5GB
```

Then, remove the license from the mailbox to eliminate the monthly charge.

```
$MSOLSKU = (Get-MSOLUser -UserPrincipalName de-
partedemployee).Licenses[0].AccountSkuId
Set-MsolUserLicense -UserPrincipalName departedem-
ployee -RemoveLicenses $MSOLSKU
```

Obtaining Last Logon Times for Office 365 Accounts

For auditing purposes, you might need to obtain statistics about the last time accounts in your tenant were accessed. You can use the LastLogonTime property of the Get-MailboxStatistics command to get this in a fairly easy way; contrast this with attempting to use the Office 365 admin portal to go through each account you have and also looking at the Exchange properties for the same information. There is not a big difference between the two methods for two or three users, but the former method would be a huge timesaver in the event you have 500 people in your tenant.

```
Get-Mailbox | Get-MailboxStatistics | Sort DisplayName
| FT -AutoSize DisplayName, LastLogonTime
```

Running that command on my small tenant takes about 20 seconds and produces the following output, just as an example:

```
WARNING: The user hasn't logged on to mailbox 'Discov-
erySearchMailbox{D919BA05-46A6-415f-80AD-7E0933
4BB852}' ('65d5e60b-1ff1-493b-830e-460478a919c8'), so
there is no data to return. After the user log
s on, this warning will no longer appear.

DisplayName              LastLogonTime
-----------              -------------
Jonathan Hassell         11/16/2015 12:09:13 PM
Salt Rose Marketing      11/16/2015 8:49:29 AM
```

Onboarding a List of New Users to Your Office 365 Tenant

In this example, we will do some scripting magic to save hours. If you regularly work with different clients, or otherwise consistently add a bunch of users to the Office 365 tenants that you manage, having an automated way of setting up these users and assigning them the appropriate licenses could save you a lot of time. PowerShell is fantastic at this type of rote work; it just asks you to assign some variables and tell it what to do with a list of things over which it can iterate. In this example, we will use a comma separated values file (CSV file) that can contain just one column: the user principal name, or UPN, of the users who you want to add. You can add other things to the file as well, such as first names and last names, but in the meat of this task we'll focus only on the UPN, which is what your users will use to log in to their Office 365 accounts this script creates. Once you are tied into Azure Active Directory within PowerShell, use the following command to get a list of the types of licenses available in your tenant.

```
Get-MsolAccountSku
```

Look on this list and find the name of the service plan (also called a SKU type or license type) you want to assign to these new users. You'll need the whole name, which might look like yourorg:ENTERPRISEPACK or something similar.

Then, import your list of users from the CSV file.

```
$UsersToAdd = Import-Csv c:\documents\listofusers.csv
```

Then connect to the Microsoft Online service with administrator credentials:
```
Connect-MSOLService
```

Then set some variables so that you can insert the SKU type you found above and the usage location into the command we will use to iterate over the list of users and create and assign their licenses:

```
$LicenseToAdd = " yourorg:ENTERPRISEPACK "
$UsageLocation = "US"
$LicenseOptions = New-MsolLicenseOptions -AccountSkuId
$LicenseToAdd
```

Finally, do the hard work by calling the Users variable, which stores the output of the CSV file, and, for each user listed in there, set the usage location and licenses.

```
$Users | ForEach-Object {
New-MsolUser -UserPrincipalName $_.UserPrincipalName
Set-MsolUser -UserPrincipalName $_.UserPrincipalName -
UsageLocation $UsageLocation
Set-MsolUserLicense -UserPrincipalName $_.UserPrinci-
palName -AddLicenses $LicenseToAdd -LicenseOptions
$LicenseOptions
}
```

Lock Down and Configure Sharing on a SharePoint Online Tenant

One of the biggest draws to Microsoft hosting SharePoint for you within Office 365 is the ability to create extranet-like functionality with a couple of clicks. For example, you can decide to share a document, document library, or even whole site access with users external to your organization without worrying (at least from the end user's perspective) about federation, identity management, mapping credentials, and all that jazz.

But for some companies, especially those with more stringent or sensitive regulatory and compliance requirements, you might want to completely disable the ability for users outside your own Office 365 tenant to have access or even receive invitations to the content stored within your tenant. One command in PowerShell turns this ability on and off.

To completely disable any kind of external sharing, use this command:

```
Set-SPOSite -Identity https://yoursite.share-
point.com/sites/thesiteyouwant -SharingCapability Dis-
abled
```

To enable both external user and also guest (i.e., unauthenticated) access, use this command:

```
Set-SPOSite -Identity https://yoursite.share-
point.com/sites/thesiteyouwant -SharingCapability Ex-
ternalUserAndGuestSharing
```

To enable only authenticated external users (not guests) to have content shared with them, use this command:

```
Set-SPOSite -Identity https://yoursite.share-
point.com/sites/thesiteyouwant -SharingCapability Ex-
ternalUserSharingOnly
```

Examining Who Has External Access to a SharePoint Online Site

Along those same lines, you might want to know the existing state of sharing on your tenant. The following commands will spit out sharing status and also who has received invitations outside your organization for each site in your tenant:

```
$SitesToAudit = Get-SPOSite | Where-Object
{$_.SharingCapability -ne Disabled}
```

```
ForEach-Object ($Site in $SitesToAudit)
{
Write-Host $Site.URL " has " $Site.SharingCapability "
configured"
Get-SPOExternalUser -SiteUrl $Site.URL | Select Dis-
playName, Email, InvitedBy, WhenCreated | Format-Table
-AutoSize
}
```

Add and Remove People from Mailing Lists (Distribution Groups)

Lots of intra-organization communication happens via distribution groups, the official Exchange and Office 365 term for mailing lists. Sometimes, however, you need to add or remove employees from different distribution groups. A couple of commands can help with that:

```
Add-DistributionGroupMember -Identity "NameOfDistribu-
tionGroup" -Member "usertoadd@yourorganization.org"
Remove-DistributionGroupMember -Identity "NameOfDis-
tributionGroup" -Member usertodelete@yourorganiza-
tion.org
```

What if you need to create a new distribution group and then add a list of users to that group? Perhaps there has been a reorganization and you need to re-create lists of direct reports, organizational hierarchy-based lists, or perhaps there is a new project happening with a lot of cross-departmental members and you need to add 50 people to a list quickly. PowerShell makes this easy. Assume you have a list of e-mail addresses in a CSV file. That file looks like this:

```
Emailaddress
user1@yourorganization.org
user2@yourorganization.org
```

and so on. Just one column, the e-mail address, is necessary unless there is more data you want to populate. Those e-mail addresses will need to already exist within your Office 365 tenant in order for this command to work.

First, we'll establish a variable to hold that:

```
$UsersToAdd = Import-CSV listofusers.csv
```

Then we'll write a simple routine that iterates over that list and pipes each e-mail address to the `Add-DistributionGroupMember` command.

```
ForEach ($User in $UsersToAdd)
{
Add-365DistributionGroupMember -Identity "Test DG" -
Member $User.emailaddress
}
```

Performing a Mass Password Change

For a variety of reasons you might be looking to change the passwords of a bunch of users all at the same time. Luckily, Azure Active Directory can randomly generate passwords so in the event of a security breach or something else time sensitive, you can use these couple of commands to lock everything down in just a few minutes.

First, export a list of users to a CSV for whom you want to change passwords. In the example below, I am selecting a department called North America and sending that output to a CSV called tochange.csv.

```
Get-MsolUser | Where { $_.department -eq "North Amer-
ica" } | select UserPrincipalName | Export-Csv .\to-
change.csv -NoTypeInformation
```

Then, use some looping magic to get the passwords changed.

```
Import-Csv .\tochange.csv | % {[string[]]$a+=
$_.UserPrincipalName + "  " + (Set-MsolUserPassword -
userPrincipalName $_.UserPrincipalName -
ForceChangePassword $True)} ;$a
```

Place All Mailboxes on Litigation Hold

Your organization may wish to preserve all e-mails and other mailbox content indefinitely for archival and regulatory compliance purposes. You can do this by enabling a feature called Litigation Hold on all of your tenants mailboxes.

No, it doesn't mean you're going to get sued: it just prevents retention policies and the managed folder algorithms from deleting e-mail once it passes certain age thresholds. This command sets all mailboxes in your tenant on hold for a period of one year (that's the 365 in the command):

```
Get-Mailbox -ResultSize Unlimited -Filter {Recipi-
entTypeDetails -eq "UserMailbox"} | Set-Mailbox -Liti-
gationHoldEnabled $true -LitigationHoldDuration 365
```

The Last Word

As I mentioned, my goal for this chapter of *Learning PowerShell* was to demonstrate how you can use PowerShell to make quick work of a bunch of rote administrative work—in this case, managing Office 365 and all its various component services, including Exchange and SharePoint.

Chapter 12
Desired State Configuration

Welcome to Chapter 12 of *Learning PowerShell*! In this chapter, we'll look at a new beast in the PowerShell world: desired state configuration, or DSC. Without further ado, let's dig in.

Understanding Desired State Configuration

The basic idea behind Desired State Configuration is that instead of configuring your own systems to be how you need them, by adding roles, installing software packages, adjusting Registry entries, configuring settings for those worker roles, and hardening the security posture of a system, you can lay out, in a series of templates, how you think your systems that perform certain functions or roles should be configured. This is your desired state. Then, when you bring a new system online, you tell PowerShell that you want it to go make this new system look like the templates you have laid out; in other words, you tell PowerShell to "make it so." And then, to the best of its ability, PowerShell goes out and, well, does it!

– The bread and butter of PowerShell DSC is a new declarative syntax that, as you might imagine, lets you declare a configuration through a series of statements. DSC pairs this new declarative syntax with a new rules engine that parses this syntax and translates those statements into the configuration rules and changes that are required to carry out your vision. There are some other moving parts to the whole system, but the syntax language and the engine are the two elements that matter the most.

– DSC can be used both to quickly bring new systems online in your desired configuration or to create consistent environments through the development, test, and production pages; and to correct the inevitable "configuration drift" that happens as production systems are online for months and years at a time and have various fixes and changes applied. Questions like "why in the world does this web server have seven versions of the .NET Framework installed?" and "A bunch of people have been added to the local administrator group on this server and I want them gone" are easily answered. A few commands and PowerShell DSC will do the heavy lifting to get back to your "known desired" state.

– You can use PowerShell DSC on any server running Windows Server 2008 R2 or later and any client running Windows 7 or later. The binaries needed to run DSC are included in Windows 8.1 and Windows Server 2012 R2; for the

DOI 10.1515/9781501506673-012

other downlevel operating systems, you will need to download the Windows Management Framework 4.0 package from Microsoft, available here: http://www.microsoft.com/download/details.aspx?id=40855

The Push and Pull Architectures

How does the configuration work? The main choice here is the overall method by which your systems gain access to the declarative configuration files. First, you choose an architecture by which PowerShell DSC will work. There are two choices: push and pull.

Push mode works by having an administrator push (you might imagine this as a shove, actually) the files containing the desired state over to target systems. Push mode is generally manually initiated; you come in and decide to push configurations to one system or another. The main advantage of this mode is simplicity: you just need your workstation, not a new server or virtual machine, and it is easy to keep your library of configuration files consistent because they are stored locally to you. It is also where most folks start with DSC. Unfortunately, this method does not scale well, since your workstation must always be online, and it does not target laptops and remote computers very well because they, too, must always be online. There are also problems with firewall configurations, too, because any of your target machines have to be configured to allow incoming connections from your workstation in order to receive the inbound files. Push mode is a good place to start testing DSC and learning how it works, but you will find the next mode will be the one you want in production.

Pull mode, on the other hand, involves a central place to store configuration—a main server, if you will—and systems are instructed to connect to that server to pull down configuration syntax files and carry out the instructions they contain. This is generally automatically initiated, in that systems will go fetch the file when they first come online and then regularly get updated at intervals you can select, because they continue to remain online on the network. Specifically, the individual nodes poll the central server and ask if configuration files are available, and if the files are there, the pull server sends the files to the nodes. Then, every 15 minutes by default, the nodes recheck for updated configuration files. All of this takes place over web services queries, so no new firewall ports have to be opened to deploy DSC in this architecture. This obviously is a better choice at scale for production use of DSC since you can manage a whole swath of machines much more easily by just having them check by themselves rather than trying to push configuration files out yourself. Of course, the big disadvantage is that it is one more server (or virtual machine; this role is not taxing from a computing hardware point of view) to manage, but in the end, I think you will save more time overall on managing tens or hundreds of even thousands of server configurations, than you will managing one additional PowerShell DSC server.

Understanding Idempotence

PowerShell DSC operates under the concept of idempotence. I don't mind telling you that when I first heard that word being used, I had no idea what it meant. Hint: it's not what Viagra cures. Idempotence refers to the concept of being able to issue the same command, or apply the same instructions, multiple times while gaining the same result each and every time. In the context of desired state configuration, it essentially means that you can run the same configuration instructions over and over again and only the parts on the target system that differ from the configurations listed in the instruction file will change; everything else will remain the same. In this way, you can simply say to DSC, "apply this whole file again," and PowerShell will apply the parts that matter and ignore the parts that are already there and fine.

More interestingly, the Idempotence property of DSC lets you add and change parts of your configuration templates at will, without having to integrate scripting logic and if/then constructs to PowerShell scripts to achieve the same result. So now if you need to tweak the version of .NET Framework your web server configuration calls for, or if you need to add or modify a Registry entry for certain server systems, you can simply make the change in your file and PowerShell DSC will apply the change as necessary--no script reworking required.

Desired State Configuration Resources

Obviously with DSC, you need to know the known universe of what you can manage--is it just Windows roles? What about other server products like System Center and Exchange? We can get the answers to those questions by examining DSC resources. A PowerShell DSC resource is simply some setting or object that you can configure through PowerShell DSC. Think of resources as the configuration service of your servers. You can see a list of all of the PowerShell DSC resources by using a simple PowerShell command:

```
Get-DSCResource | Select-Object name | Format-Table
AutoSize
```

You get the following choices on a standard system:

- **File** , where you can touch, change, and add and delete files and folders on specific targets
- **Archive** , which basically unzips a file
- **Environment** , where you can manage the environmental variables on your target (like Path and so on)
- **Group** , where you can add and remove users from groups and check their membership status
- **Log** , to write specific messages in the PowerShell DSC event log (great for troubleshooting and marking progress)
- **Package** , which installs or removes a Windows package like a Microsoft Installer (MSI) package
- **Registry** , which adds, removes, and changes registry keys except the HKEY Users registry branch
- **Script** , which simply runs a previously written PowerShell script
- **Service** , which manages the state and startup type of Windows services installed on a target node
- **User** , which manages individual user accounts (local users, not domain based accounts) on a target note
- **WindowsFeature** , which installs main Windows features like in the Add/Remove Features wizard in Server Manager
- **WindowsOptionalFeature** , which you might expect installs optional features in a similar manner
- **WindowsProcess** , which stops and starts and otherwise manages threads and processes on a target machine

As you explore DSC and start to use it in production, you will naturally want to get access to more resources. You can do this through the DSC Resource Kit, a download on Microsoft's website that adds more resource providers (think of these like PowerShell modules). You download the resource kit to your machine or centralized pull server, and then simply copy them into your PowerShell modules folder. This is probably something like C:\Windows\System32\ WindowsPowerShell\vX.X\Modules, where you replace the X.X with the version of PowerShell you're running on your system.

The Desired State Configuration Syntax

The declarative syntax is the heart of DSC and generally where you will spend the most time except for the initial setup of DSC into production in your environment. This syntax resides in simple text files which consist of five parts:

1. The key word "Configuration" followed by a label of your choosing.
2. A block of parameters used in this particular configuration.
3. A block that contains a list of nodes that this configuration should target.
4. Inside that block, the resources that this configuration file should change.
5. Nested inside the resources, which are themselves inside the node block, a list of key value pairs to indicate what about the noted resource needs to be changed by PowerShell DSC.

It might be easier to visualize how this type of file gets put together. Let's look at a simple example which simply adds the IIS role to a brand new server.

```
ConfigurationMake-IIS-Server?{ ? Node NEWSERVER1, NEWS
ERVER2? { ? WindowsFeature IIS? { ? Ensure ="Present"?
Name ="Web-Server"? }
} ?}
```

At its core, this configuration file does the following:

— The file calls itself Make-IIS-Server to distinguish it from other "templates" (this is a friendly name)
— The file has instructions that will apply to host names NEWSERVER1 and NEWSERVER2
— The file configures the IIS feature of Windows (this is also a friendly name, by the way)
— The file says to make sure the role name "Web-Server" (this is NOT a friendly name and is the required name of the IIS role that the system understands) is present on all of the systems to which this configuration file applies

That's it. You can have more than one feature block, so maybe after the IIS block, you want to add a .NET Framework block, or a PHP runtime block, or maybe you want to add the file server role to the system as well. The file can essentially contain as many feature blocks as you need.

Are you starting to see why PowerShell DSC is so cool? Instead of spending hours spelunking inside of Group Policy Object Editor windows or making System Center configuration packages, where you have to explicitly tell Windows exactly how a configuration should look like, setting by setting, with PowerShell DSC, you simply state, "this machine should be a web server with the firewall turned on," or "this machine needs the following scripts run and should never have the following roles installed" and Windows and PowerShell combined do all of the dirty work of figuring out what knobs to turn and buttons to push. Plus it is simple to copy an existing configuration file into a new text file, make some changes, and have an entirely new class of system covered by your automated configuration scheme.

The Last Word

There is a lot more to PowerShell DSC, but I hope this chapter has given you a taste of the power it brings to solve your configuration management challenges. Play around with this and see if you can figure out on your own (I hear your "no homework" screams but I've been a gentle teacher thus far!) how DSC applies and refreshes configurations and how to template out some common setups.

Chapter 13
Common Administrative Tasks with PowerShell

Sometimes it's easiest to learn something new simply by using it, and to my mind PowerShell is no exception. Often, we discover new capabilities and features in looking at tasks other people are accomplishing using PowerShell and, specifically, looking at how they're using the scripting language.

I wanted to wrap up *Learning PowerShell* with a chapter showing real-world tasks that can be accomplished using the level of PowerShell you already know based on this book. Don't get me wrong: there is a world of additional PowerShell capabilities that could fill many books, but I want to show that you now are armed with the knowledge it takes to really get some things done that are probably either already on your to-do list, or soon will be.

In this final chapter, I'll take five common tasks and show how to accomplish them using PowerShell. The tasks are:

— Adding a user
— Deleting a specific attachment (like one that contained in a virus or malware payload) from a set of Exchange mailboxes
— Handling the mailing-list deletion of employees who are leaving the company for any reason
— Working with CSV files within PowerShell
— Connecting to certain Microsoft cloud services from your on-premises servers

I will provide the commands or a script, and then I will walk you through how I put the cmdlets or scripts together so that you can see the logic of why the scripts work the way they do. You can use these as a launchpad of sorts for further customization or for creating your own daily administrative task scripts, whatever you would find useful. I hope this gives you a real taste of the practical applicability that the PowerShell scripting language can bring to your IT life.

With that said, let us get on with it!

Adding Users

Have you ever had a batch of users you needed to create accounts for, but you did not want to page through the wizards in Active Directory Users and Computers? This kind of rote, repetitive task is exactly what Windows PowerShell is designed to handle.

DOI 10.1515/9781501506673-013

```
Import-Module ActiveDirectory

Import-Csv "C:\powershell\users.csv" | ForEach-Object
{

$userPrincipal = $_."samAccountName" + "@your-
domain.local"

New-ADUser -Name $_.Name

-Path $_."ParentOU"

-SamAccountName $_."samAccountName"

-UserPrincipalName $userPrincipal

-AccountPassword (ConvertTo-SecureString "cheeseburg-
ers4all"

-AsPlainText -Force)

-ChangePasswordAtLogon $true

-Enabled $true

Add-ADGroupMember "Office Users"

$_."samAccountName";

}
```

In this script, we use the Import-CSV cmdlet, which knows how to read .CSV-formatted files. We tell the Import-CSV cmdlet that each row of the CSV data located in C:called users.csv contains information in three columns: The Name of the user; the samAccountName of the user, which is basically the login ID for the user; and the organizational unit (OU) of Active Directory that the user needs to live in.

We're also telling the cmdlet that we are using the column samAccount-Name to create the login ID for the user by marrying the value that lives in that column with the string @yourdomain.local to complete the user principal name (UPN).

From there, we loop through the file using `ForEach-Object` and send that assembled string (which is stored in the PowerShell variable called `$userPrincipal`). We assign the default password to each user as cheeseburgers4all and then set the Active Directory flag to require the user to change the password at first logon. At the end of the script, we then add all of these accounts to the Active Directory security group called Office Users.

Deleting Dangerous Content from Exchange Mailboxes

I was inspired by PowerShell MVP Mike Robbins' post (which you can find at http://mikefrobbins.com/2013/12/19/using-powershell-to-remove-phishing-emails-from-user-mailboxes-on-an-exchange-server/) on removing phishing messages from Exchange mailboxes. In this day and age I think Cryptolocker and CryptoWall ransomware infections are much more nefarious than phishing. The most recent infections go after network drives and are not well picked up and covered by client anti-malware solutions, so if you are not careful you could well pick up an infection.

For this reason, when you see a suspect message, you might want to just get it out of any mailbox it is in—a kind of mass deletion, if you will. If you are running Exchange 2010 or later, you can take care of that from within a PowerShell window.

```
Add-PSSnapin -Name Microsoft.Exchange.Management.Pow-
erShell.E2010

Get-Mailbox -ResultSize Unlimited | Search-Mailbox -
SearchQuery 'Subject:"*Please review the attached in-
voice*"' -DeleteContent | Where-Object {$_.ResultItem-
sCount}
```

In this script, we add the Exchange tools to our PowerShell window and then put two cmdlets together. The first one is a generic `Get-Mailbox` cmdlet and we also let PowerShell know that we are targeting all of the mailboxes on the system, so we tell it to give us an unlimited result size.

The second cmdlet searches the content within the mailbox and searches the subject field of every message inside each mailbox for the string we provide in the cmdlet parameter. In this case, "Please review the attached invoice" is the subject line of a Cryptolocker infection message I just received as I was writing this. The -DeleteContent eliminates the message, and the Where-Object controls the display of the results within the console window.

Before you do this, you might consider adding the -whatif parameter to this transaction so that you can see the impact of the cmdlet's intended deletion across your entire deployment. Also consider the performance implications: PowerShell searching this way is not, as we would say in the South, too terribly efficient, so for a large organization with tens of thousands of mailboxes, you can expect this operation to consume a fair amount of resources for a while.

Elegantly Handling Departed Employees and Memberships

It happens in every organization: Employees leave. They are terminated, they leave voluntarily, they get another job, they retire. Whatever the reason, you need to deal with their accounts. If your organization is like many others, users wind up embedded in tons of distribution lists per department, per project, per location, and so on.

We often find departed employee accounts still around, just without any rights or security group memberships. Most identity-lifecycle best practices suggest you should not simply delete accounts when employees leave; often, their mailboxes live on as shared resources for the remaining employees who might need to unlock some data stored within them.

However, these mailboxes can quickly fill up with distribution list messages that are completely unnecessary. So how do you keep a mailbox active but find all of its various distribution list memberships and unsubscribe from them? That's where this set of cmdlets comes in.

```
New-DistributionGroup -Name "Sayonara" -Organiza-
tionalUnit "yourdomain.local" -SamAccountName "Sayo-
nara" -Type "Security"

Import-CSV separatedemployees.csv | ForEach {Add-Dis-
tributionGroupMember -Identity "Sayonara" -Member
$_.Name}

$groupstounsubscribe=get-distributiongroup -filter
{DisplayName -ne "Sayonara"}
```

```
Get-DistributionGroupMember Sayonara | remove-distri-
butiongroupmember $groupstounsubscribe
```

First, we create a new distribution group called Sayonara, the members of which will be the accounts of departed employees. We will then procure a CSV file from human resources that lists their user principal names. We will feed that file into PowerShell, again using the `Import-CSV` cmdlet, and then say that for every entry (row) in that CSV file, we should add that login ID to the distribution group called Sayonara.

After this, we initialize a variable called `$groupstounsubscribe`. To populate this variable we ask PowerShell to get a list of all Exchange distribution groups, and then filter it down to only those in which the name is not equal to Sayonara. In other words, the lists stored in this variable will be all lists except our new Sayonara list.

In the final step of this set of cmdlets, we ask PowerShell to grab all the names within the distribution group Sayonara—the ones we want to remove from the other groups—and then pipe that list into the `remove-distribu-tiongroupmember` cmdlet using the list of groups (except Sayonara) to compare against.

What have we accomplished? All the accounts that are a member of Sayonara will get removed from any distribution group that is *not* Sayonara. So the only new mail a departed employee account's mailbox will receive is mail addressed directly to that mailbox. A neat and tidy solution.

(Hat tip to a post by David Shackelford at http://exchange-pow-ershell.com/server-management/handy-way-to-manage-distro-list-mainte-nance/.)

Create a New CSV File and Populate It with Data

This script is fairly simple but it has a number of interesting implications and is very easy to modify for your specific scenarios. We have used the `Import-CSV` cmdlet a couple of times in this chapter already, but I want to show that PowerShell can also write to CSV files as well. It's useful to get data out of a system, play around with it in Excel, and then reimport it into another cmdlet later.

```
Get-Mailbox | Select-Object Name,OrganizationalU-
nit,WindowsEmailAddress | Export-CSV C:\powershell\ex-
port.csv
```

In this case, what we are doing is using the Exchange `Get-Mailbox` cmdlet to get a list of all mailboxes on a deployment. We will pipe that output to the `Select-Object` cmdlet, which grabs specific parts of whatever it is sent; in this case we are getting the name, organizational unit and default email address properties of each mailbox. And then we are piping just those properties over to the `Export-CSV` cmdlet, which will write them conveniently to the CSV file at the directory path I included above.

If you are wondering how you can easily grab all the properties you can use within a CSV, use a get cmdlet and format the output as a list. For example, `get-mailbox jhassell | format-list` will show you all of the different properties you can use with the `Select-Object` cmdlet in the example above to populate the columns in your CSV file.

Easily Connect to Office 365 from Your Hybrid Deployment

If you are running a hybrid Exchange deployment, chances are you are connecting to the Office 365 portal a lot. If you've tried to do a lot of administrative work with PowerShell in this scenario, you know it is a bit of a rigmarole to set up the remoting necessary to run PowerShell cmdlets against the Office 365 servers. Below, I've created a script that takes care of the setup for you, so that when you are ready to go, you just run the script and enter your Office 365 administrative credentials.

```
$URL = "https://ps.outlook.com/powershell"

$Credentials = Get-Credential -Message "Enter your Exchange Online or Office 365 administrator credentials"

$CloudSession = New-PSSession -ConfigurationName Microsoft.Exchange -ConnectionUri $URL -Credential $Credentials -Authentication Basic -AllowRedirection -Name "Office 365/Exchange Online"

Import-PSSession $CloudSession Prefix 365
```

First off, we declare a variable to store the location on the Internet where we're sending all of these cmdlets—think of it like a web service. Then, we set up a variable to securely hold our username and password. The `Get-Credential` cmdlet pops up a window where you can enter credentials, and the variable will hold those credentials as secure strings. The third variable starts a new PowerShell remoting session using the specific remoting language necessary to connect up to Office 365 or Exchange Online (this works for both offerings). Finally, the `Import-PSSession` merges that session with your current console, letting you work directly within it.

This particular script is specific to hybrid deployments because sometimes namespaces for cmdlets collide. PowerShell does not always know immediately how to sort out—say, if you ran `New-Mailbox`—whether you wanted to create that new mailbox on your local deployment or in the cloud.

To fix this, the script loads the Office 365 namespace of cmdlets with the prefix `365`. So all Exchange cmdlets that should run in the cloud should use the `365` prefix, a la `New-365Mailbox` or `Get-365DistributionGroup`. All Exchange cmdlets that should run on your local deployment should be left as they are by default. This makes it very easy to distinguish one from the other.

If you want to run this script in a purely cloud environment, however, you can just remove the prefix `365` from the last line of the script and everything will return to its default.

Remember, to save this as a script, just put the cmdlets above into a text file and save the file with an extension of `.PS1`. Then, from the PowerShell console window, type in `.\script.ps1` (that's period, backslash, name of file) to run the script.

Appendix X
Quick Cheat Sheet of PowerShell Verbs

Review this quick cheat sheet of verbs. There are cmdlets that do all of these actions to a variety of nouns. PowerShell is consistent across products, so Exchange cmdlets can export and convert, and so can Office 365 and System Center cmdlets. Become familiar with these verbs so you have a starting point when you're using PowerShell with a new product or service.

Add
Clear
Convert
Copy
Export
Format
Get
Import
Invoke
Measure
Move
New
Out
Remove
Set
Start
Stop
Update
Write

DOI 10.1515/9781501506673-014

Index

Made in United States
North Haven, CT
07 October 2022

25112219R00122